Primary Christmas Concerts

by
Carol Ogilvy
and
Trudy Tinkham

illustrated by Vanessa Filkins

Cover by Vanessa Filkins

Copyright © Good Apple, Inc.

ISBN No. 0-86653-485-7

Printing No. 987654321

GOOD APPLE, INC.
BOX 299
CARTHAGE, IL 62321-0299

The purchase of this book entitles the buyer to reproduce student activity pages for classroom use only. Any other use requires written permission from Good Apple, Inc.

All rights reserved. Printed in the United States of America.

Table of Contents

A Heart-ful Present-ation 1
    (designed for one kindergarten or grade 1 class)

A Wintry Snow Show 15
    (designed for one or two kindergarten or grade 1 classes)

A Tree-mendous Christmastime 31
    (designed for one or two grade 2 or grade 3 classes)

A Fanta-sea Christmas 49
    (designed for two, three or four primary classes)

An International Christmas 70
    (designed for a large primary grouping)

Foreword

Dear Professional Colleague,

Primary Christmas Concerts consists of five primary theme-based Christmas concerts ranging from an easy kindergarten or grade 1 individual classroom concert to a more challenging Christmas presentation for a large primary class grouping to be presented in a gymnasium or auditorium.

Each concert contains:

1. a concert synopsis
2. suggestions for assigning parts
3. a time chart to help the teacher organize valuable teaching time
4. songs which are sung to the tune of familiar Christmas songs
5. suggested actions for each song
6. staging ideas
7. costume ideas
8. suggestions for programs and invitations
9. decoration ideas
10. refreshment ideas

We would like to emphasize that our book is very flexible and can be easily adapted to fit your own teaching assignment. You may wish to use our concerts in their entirety, or you may choose to do specific songs and a few ideas you are comfortable with. Please feel free to use our ideas to help make your classroom Christmas a happy event.

One teaching aid that we, as elementary teachers, find invaluable is the overhead projector. Transparency sheets of desired teaching materials can be made by either copying by hand on the transparency sheets or by using a photocopy machine to make overhead transparencies. Then these transparency sheets can be put on the overhead and projected onto a screen or chalkboard to make a larger copy of your desired teaching material. For instance, to learn new Christmas song lyrics, we suggest you use the overhead projector to project the new song on a screen for a group of children to see. This allows for all your students to focus together on one source for the specific lines of the song, and it eliminates the rustling of song sheets by "little fingers."

Many of our art ideas for *Primary Christmas Concerts* make use of the overhead projector. To do this:

1. obtain a specific picture which needs to be enlarged
2. make an overhead transparency of the picture
3. shine the projector onto large heavy school paper which has been taped to a chalkboard or a firm surface
4. trace the picture with a pencil onto the paper
5. turn off projector
6. paint or decorate the picture, outline it in black paint or black felt pen and cut out
7. paint large sections of paper for optional scenery

So, if at all possible, make yourself familiar with the overhead projector. It is a useful teaching aid for all subject areas.

Our songs for each concert are all tunes of familiar Christmas songs and carols. Our favorite piano music book is *John Lane's Christmas Friends* published by United Artists. All the songs in our concert book can be found in this piano book. If you are not musical, we suggest you get a friend or colleague to play the concert music for you and then you can tape it. The students can easily learn the concert songs with the aid of a classroom tape recorder.

We hope you will enjoy *Primary Christmas Concerts* and use it to its fullest. Putting on a Christmas concert need not be a "panic station task" but rather a "merry" cultural experience for one and all to thoroughly enjoy.

Best regards,
Carol Ogilvy
Trudy Tinkham

A Heart-ful Present-ation

(for one kindergarten or grade 1 class)

This primary Christmas concert is designed for one kindergarten or grade 1 class. Its theme revolves around the gift of love at Christmastime and will last approximately four to six minutes.

The concert begins with the entire group reciting a poem. Then the children will be divided into four groups and each group will sing a song. A present should be placed in front of each group. Following each song, one student from the group will open a present (which has been positioned in front of his/her group). Each present will contain one of the letters of the word LOVE (not in a specific order). The child will hold up the letter, show it to the audience and then carefully mount it on a portable or stationary bulletin board. Eventually, at the end of verse 4, the audience will see the word LOVE in its entirety in front of them, and the children will conclude their short concert with the oral recitation about the word LOVE and how it is related to their special parents.

Decorations, invitations and refreshments all revolve around the gift of love so that the entire concert will definitely turn out to be a Heart-ful Present-ation for one and all to heart-ily enjoy!

Copyright © 1989, Good Apple, Inc.

Concert Format
1. Beginning poem
2. Song (4 verses and finale)
3. Concluding oral recitation

KEY:
P — PRESENT

Staging

| BULLETIN BOARD |
| Group 2 XXXXXX   Group 3 XXXXXX |
| Group 1 XXXXXX P   P   Group 4 XXXXXX P |

AUDIENCE

Beginning Poem
(all children say poem in unison while standing)

Thank you for coming to our show.
We hope it will make your hearts glow,
Because Christmastime is filled with love,
And that's what you're so deserving of!

Song #1

The Special Letters
(sung to the tune of "Suzy Snowflake")

Verse 1

Group 1 children remain standing while other children sit down until it is their turn to sing.

(from beginning of song)

We are the first presents,
Look at how nice we are.
We start with the letter *E*, you see,
Like 'lectric trains and cars.
We are the first presents,
So open us real fast.
You'll like what you see inside our box,
At Christmas it's a blast!

When verse 1 is finished, one child opens present in front of group 1, shows the audience the letter *E* and mounts it on the bulletin board.

Actions

We are the first presents,
(raise 1 finger to indicate being first)

Look at how nice we are.
(both hands outstretched to audience)

We start with the letter *E*, you see,
(point to headband)

Like 'lectric trains and cars.
(point to picture on self)

We are the first presents,
(raise 1 finger to indicate being first)

So open us real fast.
(roll hands one on top of each other)

You'll like what you see inside our box,
(hands outstretched to audience)

At Christmas it's a blast!
(both hands raised above head)

Costumes

Children wear garbage bags with neckholes and armholes cut out. Enlarge pictures of electric toys and attach to front of garbage bags. Make a headband from white construction paper. Attach red hearts, green holly and the letter *E*.

Prop: 1 wrapped box for present with the *E* inside

GARBAGE BAG

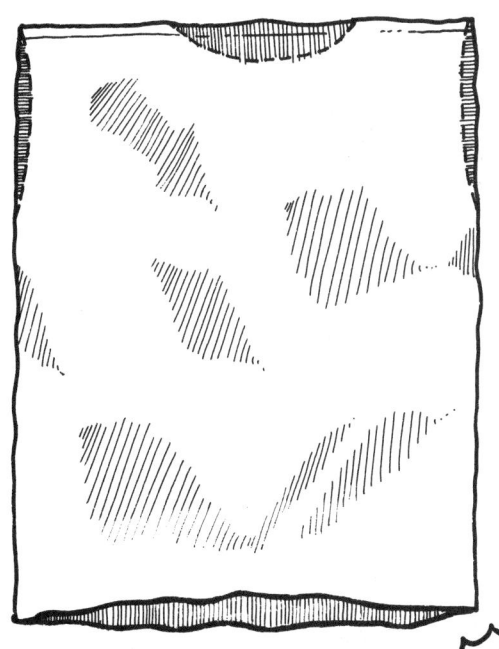

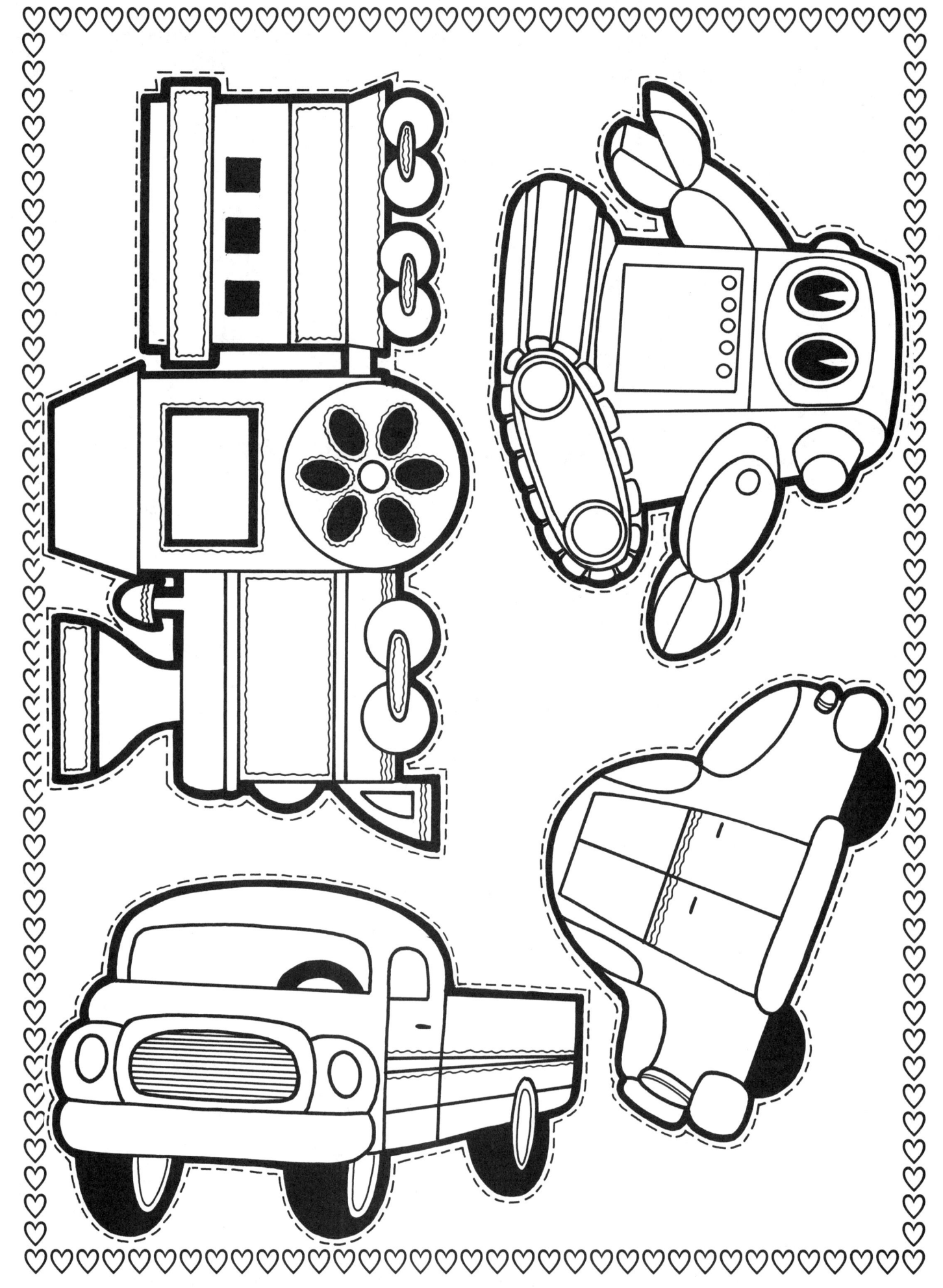

Verse 2

Group 2 children stand while other children remain in a sitting position.

(back to beginning of song)

We are the next presents,
We're filled with excitement.
We start with the letter O, you see,
Like Christmas ornaments.
We are the next presents,
So open us real fast.
You'll like what you see inside our box,
At Christmas it's a blast!

When verse 2 is finished, one child opens present in front of group 2, shows the audience the letter O and mounts it on the bulletin board.

Actions

We are the next presents,
(raise 2 fingers to indicate being second)

We're filled with excitement.
(both hands outstretched to audience)

We start with the letter O, you see,
(point to headband)

Like Christmas ornaments.
(point to picture on self)

We are the next presents,
(raise 2 fingers)

So open us real fast.
(roll hands over each other)

You'll like what you see inside our box,
(hands outstretched to audience)

At Christmas it's a blast!
(both hands raised above head)

Costumes

Children wear garbage bags with neckholes and armholes cut out. Enlarge pictures of Christmas ornaments and paint. Attach to front of garbage bags. Make a headband from white construction paper. Attach red hearts, green holly and the letter O.

Prop: 1 wrapped box with the letter O inside

Copyright © 1989, Good Apple, Inc.

Verse 3

Group 3 children stand while other children remain in a sitting position.

(back to beginning of song)

We are the third presents,
At this nice time of year.
We start with the letter V, you see,
Like very nice sports gear.
We are the third presents,
So open us real fast.
You'll like what you see inside our box,
At Christmas it's a blast!

When verse 3 is finished, one child opens present in front of group 3, shows the audience the letter V and mounts it on the bulletin board.

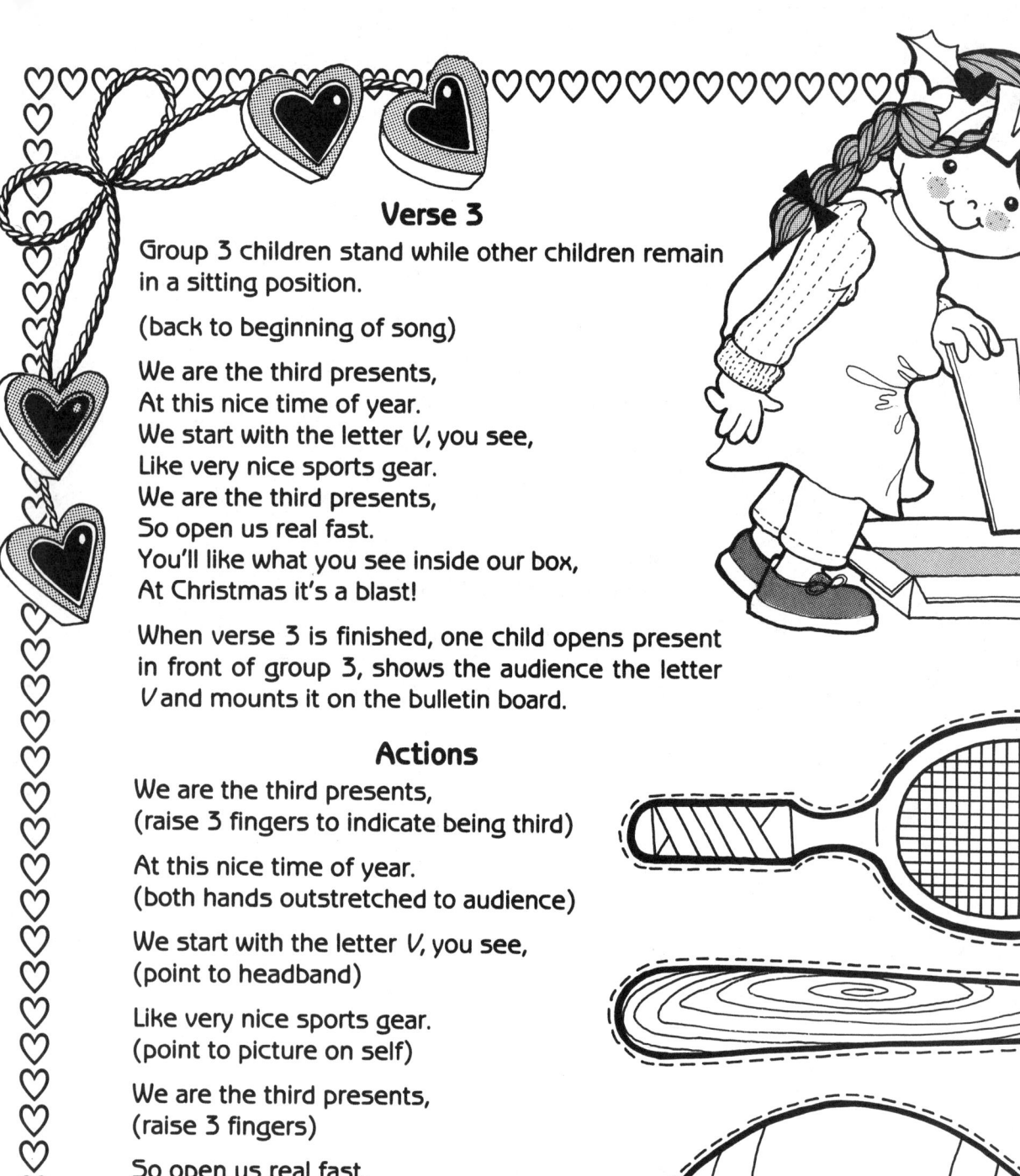

Actions

We are the third presents,
(raise 3 fingers to indicate being third)

At this nice time of year.
(both hands outstretched to audience)

We start with the letter V, you see,
(point to headband)

Like very nice sports gear.
(point to picture on self)

We are the third presents,
(raise 3 fingers)

So open us real fast.
(roll hands one on top of the other)

You'll like what you see inside our box,
(hands outstretched to audience)

At Christmas it's a blast!
(both hands raised above head)

Costumes

Children wear garbage bags with neckholes and armholes cut out. Enlarge pictures of sports gear and attach to front of garbage bag. Make a headband from white construction paper. Attach red hearts, green holly and the letter V.

Prop: 1 wrapped box for present with the letter V inside

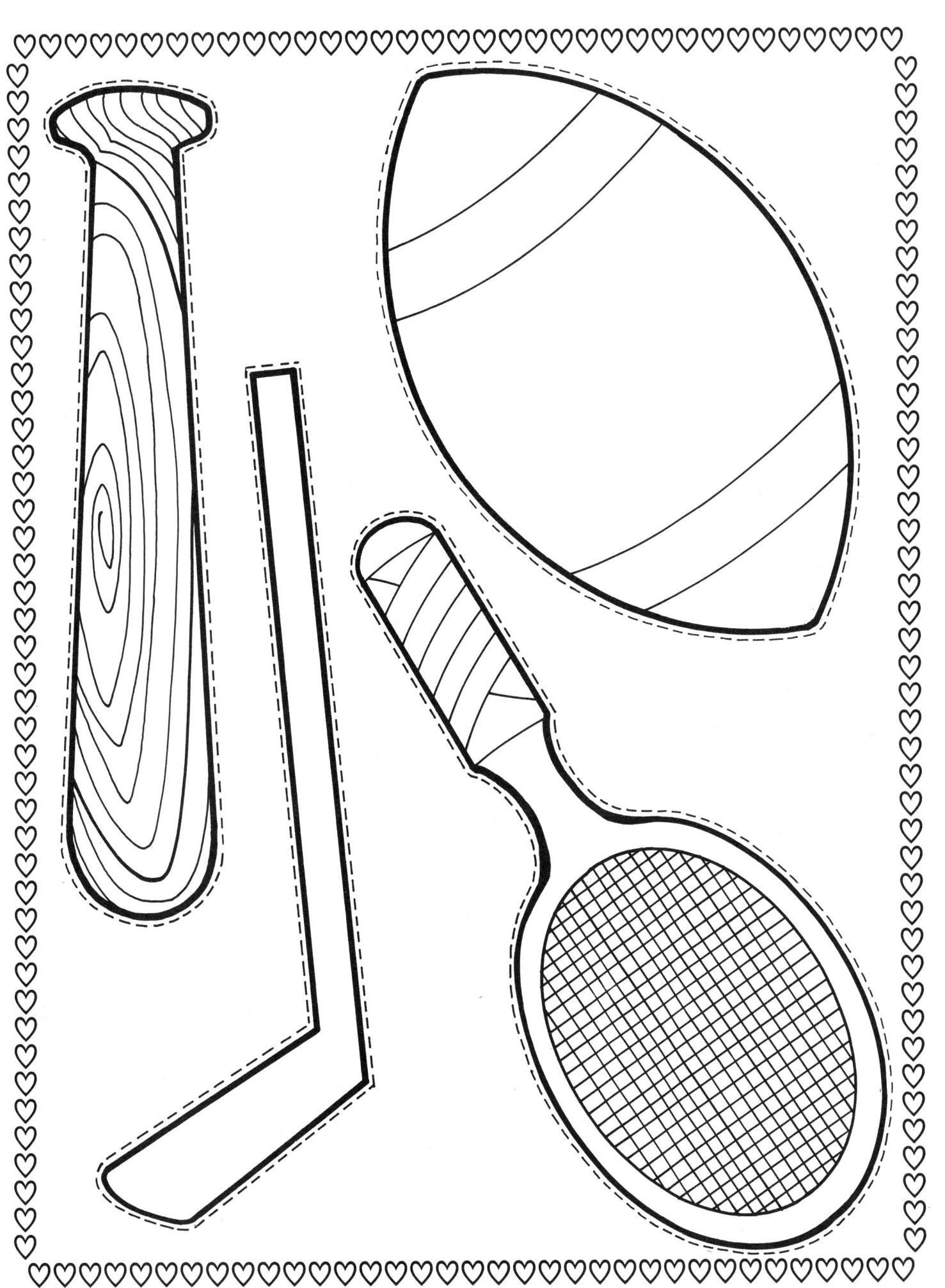

Verse 4

Group 4 children stand while other children remain in a sitting position.

(back to beginning of song)

We are the fourth presents,
Shiny and bright are we,
We start with the letter *L*, you see,
Like lights upon your tree.
We are the fourth presents,
So open us real fast.
You'll like what you see inside our box,
At Christmas it's a blast!

When verse 4 is finished, one child opens present in front of group 4, shows the audience the letter *L* and mounts it on the bulletin board.

Actions

We are the fourth presents,
(raise 4 fingers to indicate being fourth)

Shiny and bright are we,
(both hands outstretched to audience)

We start with the letter *L*, you see,
(point to headband)

Like lights upon your tree.
(point to picture on self)

We are the fourth presents,
(raise 4 fingers)

So open us real fast.
(roll hands one on top of the other)

You'll like what you see inside our box,
(hands outstretched to audience)

At Christmas it's a blast!
(both hands raised above head)

Costumes

Children wear garbage bags with neckholes and armholes cut out. Enlarge picture of Christmas tree light and attach to front of garbage bag. Make a headband from white construction paper. Attach red hearts, green holly and the letter *L*.

Prop: 1 wrapped box for present with the letter *L* inside

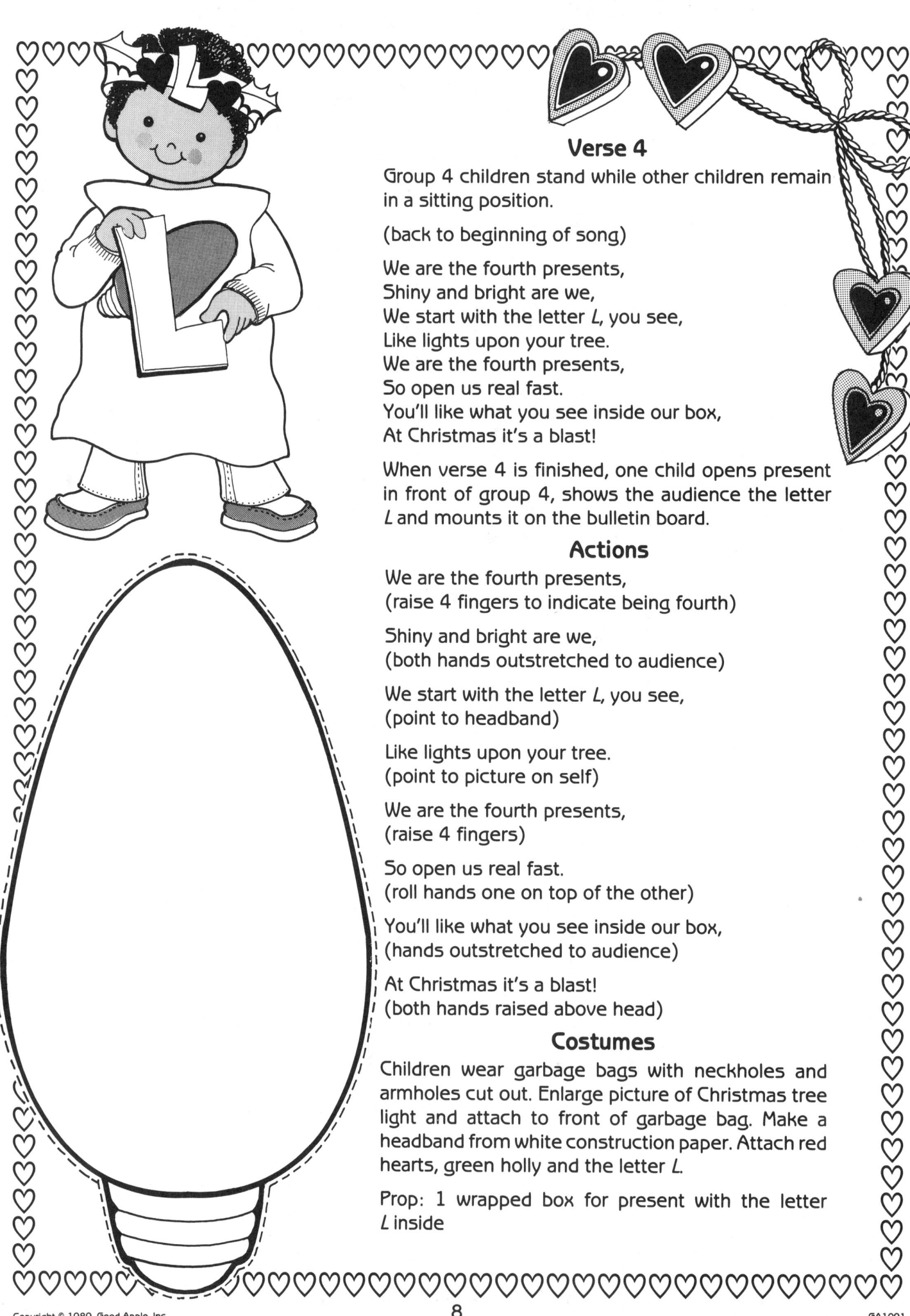

Song Finale
(sung to the tune of "Suzy Snowflake")

(start at the line "If you wanna. . .")

We all stand for special letters,
L-O-V-E is what we spell.
We all stand for special letters,
LOVE is great to tell.
We are all the presents
Standing in front of you.
We spell L-O-V-E, yes, that's LOVE,
Merry Christmas, too!

Actions

We all stand for special letters,
(each group joins hands)

L-O-V-E is what we spell.
(drop hands, point to headbands)

We all stand for special letters,
(each group joins hands)

LOVE is great to tell.
(drop hands, point to headbands)

We are all the presents
(both hands point to self)

Standing in front of you.
(both hands outstretched to audience)

We spell L-O-V-E, yes, that's LOVE,
(point to bulletin board)

Merry Christmas, too!
(both hands outstretched to audience)

Staging

Before song, all children stand and go into practiced formation of groups of four so that the headbands spell out the word LOVE. They remain standing while they sing the finale.

Concluding Oral Recitation

Children remain standing in L-O-V-E group formations. They all turn to face the bulletin board, then back to the audience and say the following recitation led by the teacher.

L—L is for the bright light that flickers in your heart
O—O is for the open mind you've had from the start
V—V is for the valuable lessons you teach me
E—E is for the times we've spent entertainingly

When the recitation is finished, the children bow and sit down on the floor. At this time the teacher may announce points of information he/she has and then invite the audience to join in for refreshments at the refreshment table.

Invitations

Teacher fills out pertinent information on invitation and duplicates enough copies for each child. Children decorate them. Send home the first week of December.

← fold

A Heart-ful Christmas Present-ation!

← fold

Please come to our

Heart-ful Christmas Present-ation!

Date: _____ Time: _____
Place: _____
Given by: _____ R.S.V.P. by: _____
A HEART-Y lunch will follow our concert.

For our refreshments after the concert, we would heart-ily appreciate your sending _____
_____
the day before the concert.

fold →

Programs

1. Fill in pertinent information.
2. Duplicate one program for each concert guest.
3. Have students color programs.
4. Designate two students to hand out programs with name tags.

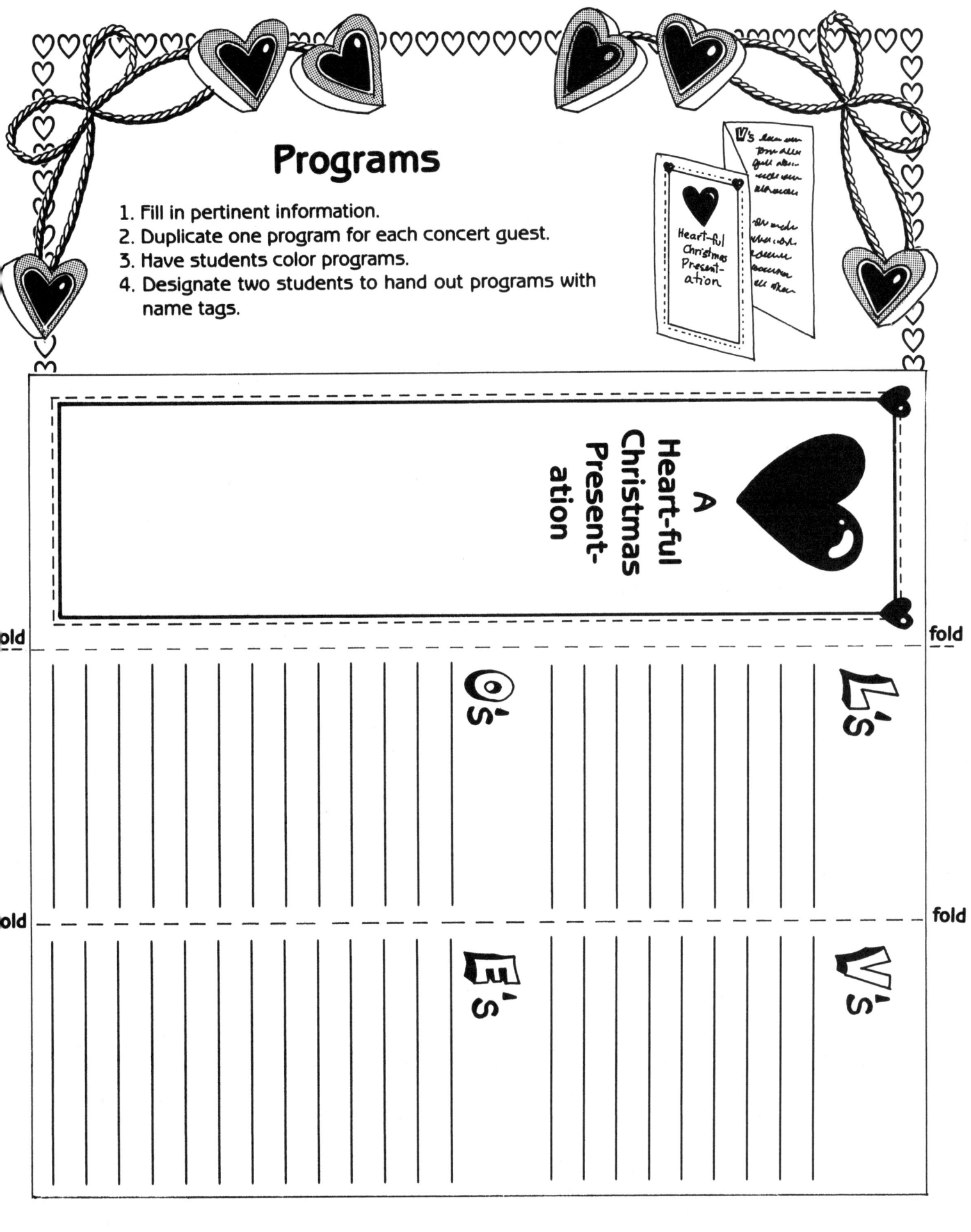

Decorations

Bulletin Board
Cover bulletin board with green mural paper. Cut out holly from green construction paper. Cut out hearts from red construction paper. Staple holly and hearts to the corners of the bulletin board.

Door Decoration
WELCOME TO OUR "HEART-WARMING" CHRISTMAS HAPPENING!

Cut out large red heart from mural paper. Decorate with green holly cut from construction paper. Print words in large block letters with black felt pen.

Name Tags
Teacher enlarges name tags and duplicates enough for each guest. Children decorate outside edges and cut them out. When parents and/or invited guests arrive, they individually print their own names on the name tags and pin them on.

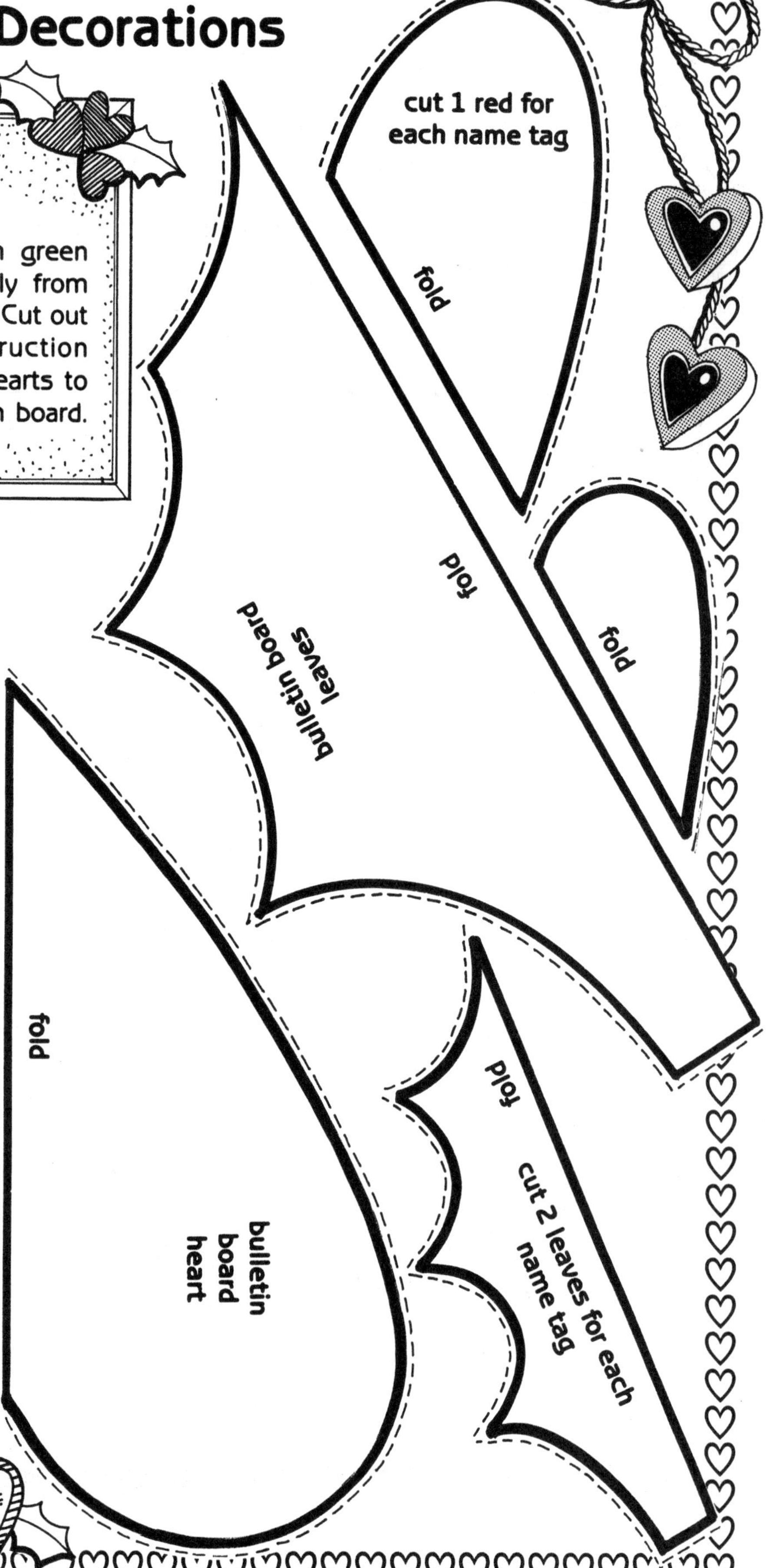

cut 1 red for each name tag
fold
fold
bulletin board leaves
bulletin board heart
fold
fold
cut 2 leaves for each name tag

Refreshments

1. On the invitations parents are asked to bring or send one of the following items to school the day before the concert:
   paper cups
   napkins
   wrapping paper
   sandwiches individually wrapped in plastic wrap
   oranges
   miniature candy canes
   shoe boxes (one for each student and guest)
2. The week of the concert, the teacher has parent helpers or students make heart-shaped sugar cookies and decorate them with a variety of icings. Wrap each cookie individually.
3. The morning of the concert, parent helpers fill the shoe boxes with above items for individual lunches (for each guest and each student). The final item that is placed in each box is a construction paper heart. The boxes are then sealed and wrapped in Christmas wrapping paper.
4. After the concert is over, the teacher invites everyone to help themselves to a heart-y lunch. Each person obtains one box for his/her lunch from a central table. Tea, coffee and a red punch (with cherry ice cubes) should also be on the table for lunchtime beverages.

Heart-ful THANKS for coming to our concert. Merry Christmas!

Time Chart

This chart will allow you to plan in advance the music and art activities required for "A Heart-ful Present-ation."

Songs and Actions	8 music sessions before concert
Poem Recitation	4 oral reading sessions
Practicing Entire Concert	2 sessions before concert
Costumes	2 art sessions or have parents make them
Decorations	6 art sessions—display when complete
Invitations	1 art session—send home the same day
Programs	1 art session—delegate one or two students to hand out programs at the door on the day of the concert.
Cookies	1 cultural session the week of the concert

Day of Concert dress rehearsal
hang door decoration
set up chairs for audience
set up benches and bulletin board for children's performance
parent helpers fill refreshment boxes
set up refreshment table

A WINTRY SNOW SHOW

(for one or two kindergarten or grade 1 classes)

This very simple Christmas concert is designed for one or two kindergarten or grade 1 classes. It consists of four songs and one recitation poem. Each student learns and sings all four songs. He learns the actions to his designated part. If you plan to do the concert in its entirety, the students are to learn all the concert songs. Each group will come forward and do their actions for their song. This concert is adaptable because you can delete songs if need be, that is if you are part of a schoolwide presentation and have only three or four minutes for your part of the concert.

The following is a guideline for assigning parts:

Characters	1 Classes	2 Classes
Icicles	7	13
Snowflakes	6	12
Snowballs	6	12
Snowmen	6	13

Time Chart

This time chart will allow you to plan in advance the art and music activities required for "A Wintry Snow Show."

Songs and Actions	10 music sessions before concert
Poem Recitation	4 oral reading sessions
Practicing Entire Concert	2 sessions before concert
Dress Rehearsal	morning of concert
Costumes	2 art sessions or have parent helpers make them
Decorations	5 art sessions—display when complete 1 session for snowflakes 1 session for icicles 2 sessions for bulletin board 1 session for felt ornaments
Invitations	1 art session—send home the same day
Programs	1 art session—delegate one or two students to hand out programs at the door on the day of the concert.
Concert Setup	On day of concert hang door decoration. Set up benches for children to stand on and chairs for guests to sit on. Set up refreshment table.

Song #1

We're Icicles
(sung to the tune of "O Christmas Tree")

We're icicles, we're icicles,
We're wintertime Popsicles.
We're icicles, we're icicles,
We hang from your windowsills.
We're very long and shiny too,
We like to melt when sky is blue.
We're icicles, we're icicles,
We're wintertime Popsicles.

Actions

We're icicles, we're icicles,
(point to self two times)

We're wintertime Popsicles.
(pretend to shiver)

We're icicles, we're icicles,
(point to self two times)

We hang from your windowsills.
(point to audience)

We're very long and shiny too,
(using both hands, make icicles in a V shape)

We like to melt when sky is blue.
(middle child pretends to melt to the ground)

We're icicles, we're icicles,
(point to self two times)

We're wintertime Popsicles.
(turn around so audience can see Popsicles on the backs of students)

Costumes

Body: Use a white garbage bag and slit open the bottom fold, weave ribbon or garland through top and bottom so it may be gathered around child's neck and knees. Cut armholes. Stuff shoulders with newspaper.

Head: Attach Br-r-r sign to winter toques.

Popsicles: Overhead shape, cut out and attach to back of icicle costume.

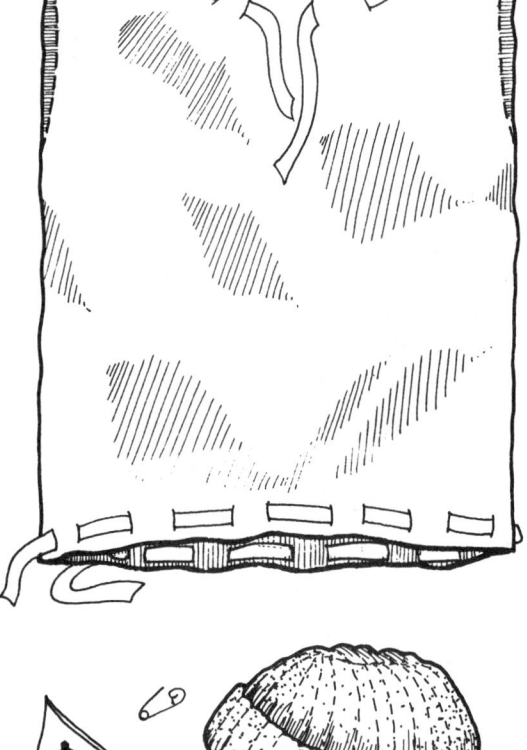

Staging

Each group sits on separate benches and takes their place when it is time for them to sing. Icicles leave their bench before song and take their stage position. After song they return to their original position on the bench.

```
  XXXXXXX        SSSSSS         oooooo         MMMMMM  ←
  ICICLES       SNOWFLAKES      SNOWBALLS      SNOWMEN
                                                         BENCHES
       X            X                              X
                           X    X
                                AUDIENCE
```

Song #2
Snowflakes
(sung to the tune of "Jingle Bells")

Chorus:
Snowflakes here, snowflakes there,
Snowflakes everywhere,
Falling here and falling there,
We sure don't stay in the a-air.
Snowflakes here, snowflakes there,
Snowflakes all around
Drifting here and drifting there
And then falling on the ground.

Actions

Snowflakes here, snowflakes there,
(point to right, point to left)

Snowflakes everywhere,
(point to audience)

Falling here and falling there,
We sure don't stay in the a-air.
(wiggle fingers from above head and move in a downward motion)

Snowflakes here, snowflakes there,
(with right arm make large circle clockwise)

Snowflakes all around
(circle pattern in front of body)

Drifting here and drifting there
(drift out of position)

And then falling on the ground.
(pretend to slowly drift to ground)

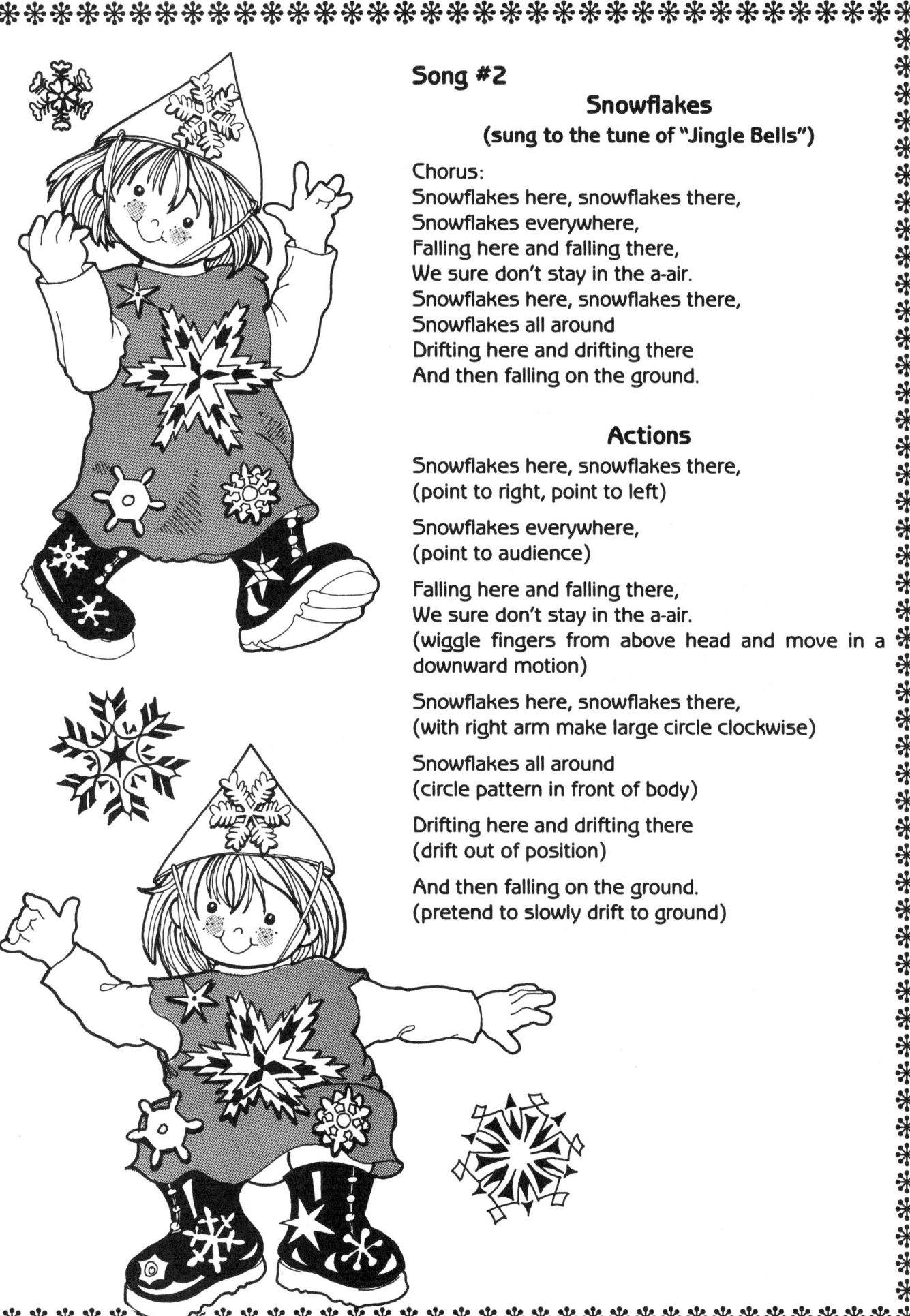

Costumes

Body: Green garbage bag with neck and armholes cut out. Cut different sizes of white snowflakes and tape all over front and back of garbage bag.

Head: Make cone-shaped hat out of construction paper and tape small snowflakes onto it. Secure hat with elastic around chin.

Optional: Small snowflakes taped onto winter boots, winter gloves, or even cheeks.

Staging

Before song, Snowflakes leave benches and take their stage position. After song, they return to their places on the benches.

XXXXXXX	SSSSSS	OOOOOO	MMMMMM
ICICLES	**SNOWFLAKES**	**SNOWBALLS**	**SNOWMEN**

S   S   S   S   S   S

AUDIENCE

Song #3

Snowballs
(sung to the tune of "Up on the Housetop")

Out in the front yard the snow falls down;
We rush out in one great bound.
We want to make lots of cold snowballs,
Shape them and throw them to one and all.
Throw, throw, throw! It's just some snow.
Throw, throw, throw! It's just some snow.
Out in the front yard, pack, pack, pack,
Hide behind a tree 'cuz we'll at-tack!

Actions

Out in the front yard the snow falls down;
(look upwards, arms bent from elbow, palms pointing up)

We rush out in one great bound.
(run on spot)

We want to make lots of cold snowballs,
Shape them and throw them to one and all.
(bend down, pretend to scoop up snow with both hands)

Throw, throw, throw! It's just some snow.
(pretend to throw snowballs at each other)

Throw, throw, throw! It's just some snow.
(pretend to throw snow at people on benches)

Out in the front yard, pack, pack, pack,
(same as line 1) (cup hand, place the other over it and twist three times)

Hide behind a tree 'cuz we'll at-tack!
(Put hands in two side pockets. Get out two Styrofoam balls which are hiding in pockets and gently throw out into audience.)

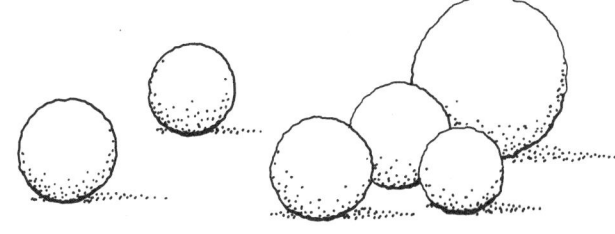

21

Copyright © 1989, Good Apple, Inc.

GA1091

Costumes

Body: Each child wears a winter coat, a toque, mittens, scarf and boots.

Optional: Tack garland on winter outfit with safety pins or running needle stitch if desired.

Prop: Two Styrofoam balls for each student

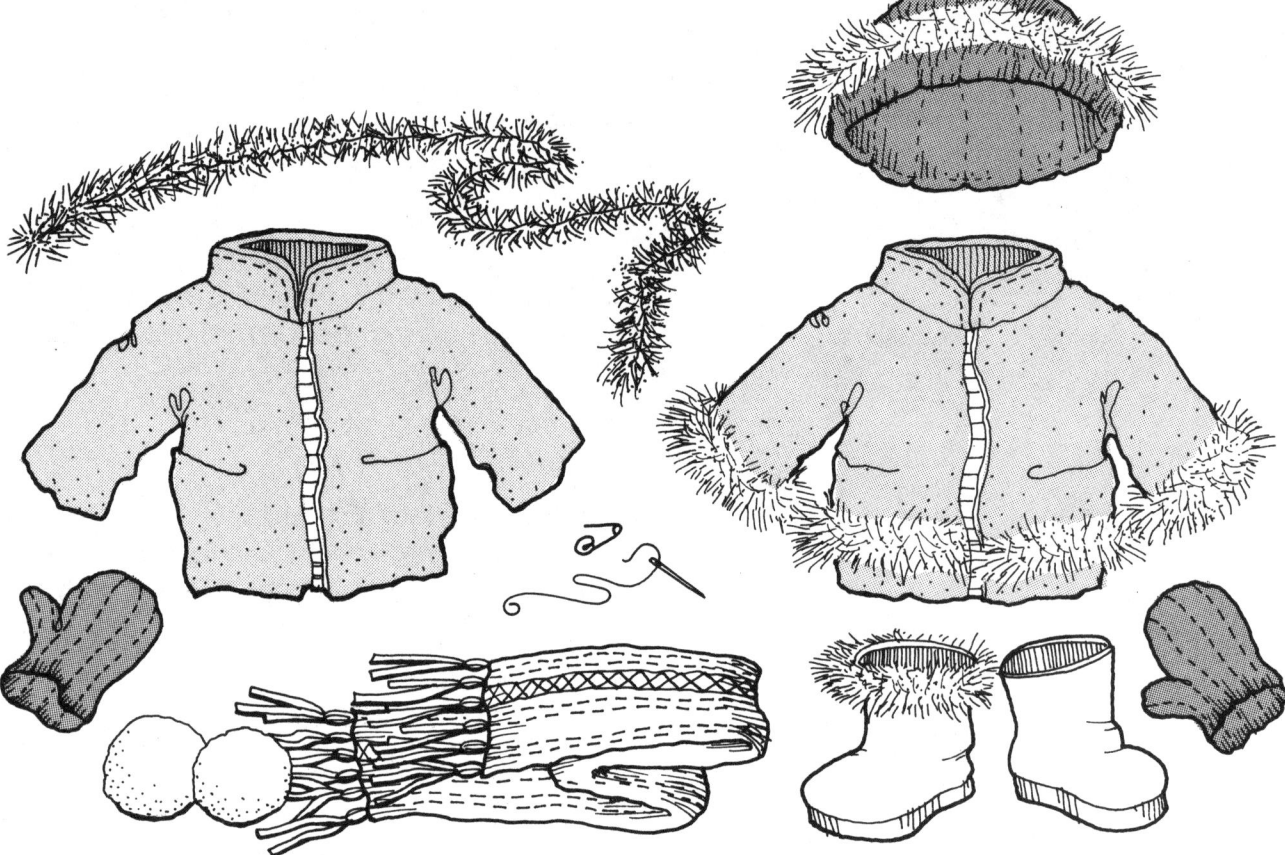

Staging

Before song, Snowballs leave their bench and take their stage position. After song, they return to their original place on their bench.

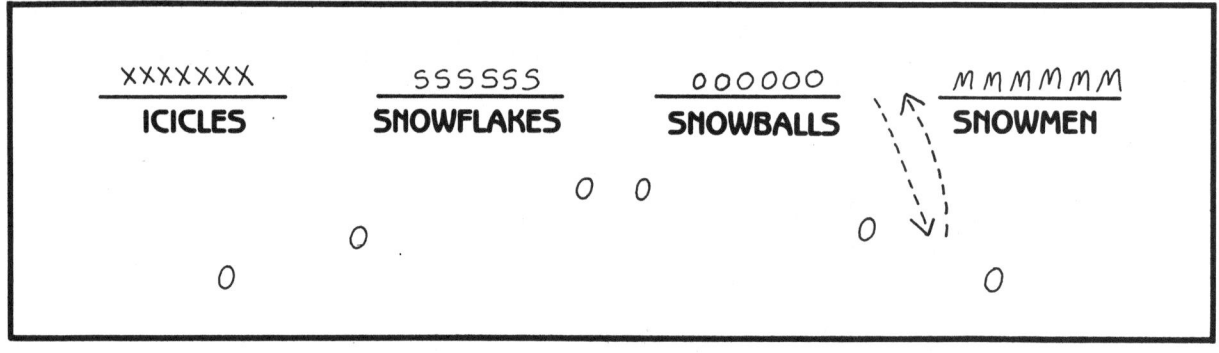

Song #4

Snowmen
(sung to the tune of "Deck the Halls")

We're a bunch of jolly snowmen!
Ho-ho-ho-ho-ho! We're made of snow!
In the winter we have such fun!
Ho-ho-ho-ho-ho! We're made of snow!
Jolly and fat, yes we are that!
Ho-ho-ho-ho-ho! We're made of snow!
Dad's old pipe and a black top hat!
Ho-ho-ho-ho-ho! We're made of snow!

Actions

We're a bunch of jolly snowmen!
(put left hand on hip, shake right index finger at audience)

Ho-ho-ho-ho-ho! We're made of snow!
(make large circle in front of body with hands and arms, pretend to jiggle fat tummy)

In the winter we have such fun!
(with right index finger, trace happy face on mouth—back and forth)

Ho-ho-ho-ho-ho! We're made of snow!
(repeat line 2)

Jolly and fat, yes we are that!
(sway from side to side)

Ho-ho-ho-ho-ho! We're made of snow!
(repeat line 2)

Dad's old pipe and a black top hat!
(point to mouth, then to hat)

Ho-ho-ho-ho-ho! We're made of snow!
(repeat line 2)

Costume

Head: Each child wears a black top hat and a scarf around neck.

Body: From heavyweight white cardboard, cut two circles, staple together and paint buttons down the middle. Secure to neck with string. Trim with garland. Wear winter boots on feet.

Face: Rouge on cheeks.

Staging

Before song, Snowmen leave their bench and take their stage position. After song, they return to their original position on their bench.

xxxxxxx	sssss	ooooo	mmmmm
ICICLES	**SNOWFLAKES**	**SNOWBALLS**	**SNOWMEN**
M	M	M	
M	M	M	M

AUDIENCE

Poem

(choral recitation by all members)
(Staging position for poem: Icicles, Snowflakes, Snowballs and Snowmen stand in front of their benches to recite poem.)

Snowflakes, snowmen and icicles too,
We even had snowballs for you.
Winter is fun, that you know;
Thanks for coming to our "Snow Show."

MERRY CHRISTMAS!

(Everyone files off stage.)

Actions

Snowflakes, snowmen and icicles too,
(Snowflakes wave, then Snowmen wave, then Icicles wave)

We even had snowballs for you.
(Snowballs wave)

Winter is fun, that you know;
(point to audience with right index finger)

Thanks for coming to our "Snow Show."
(Hands outstretched to audience)

MERRY CHIRSTMAS!
(All characters wave to audience.)

Invitations

1. With teacher's help, each child will cut out a white snowflake pattern from 8½" x 11" paper.
2. Mount snowflake pattern on dark-blue construction paper.
3. Duplicate invitation information on light-blue paper. Cut out circle and paste onto white snowflake.

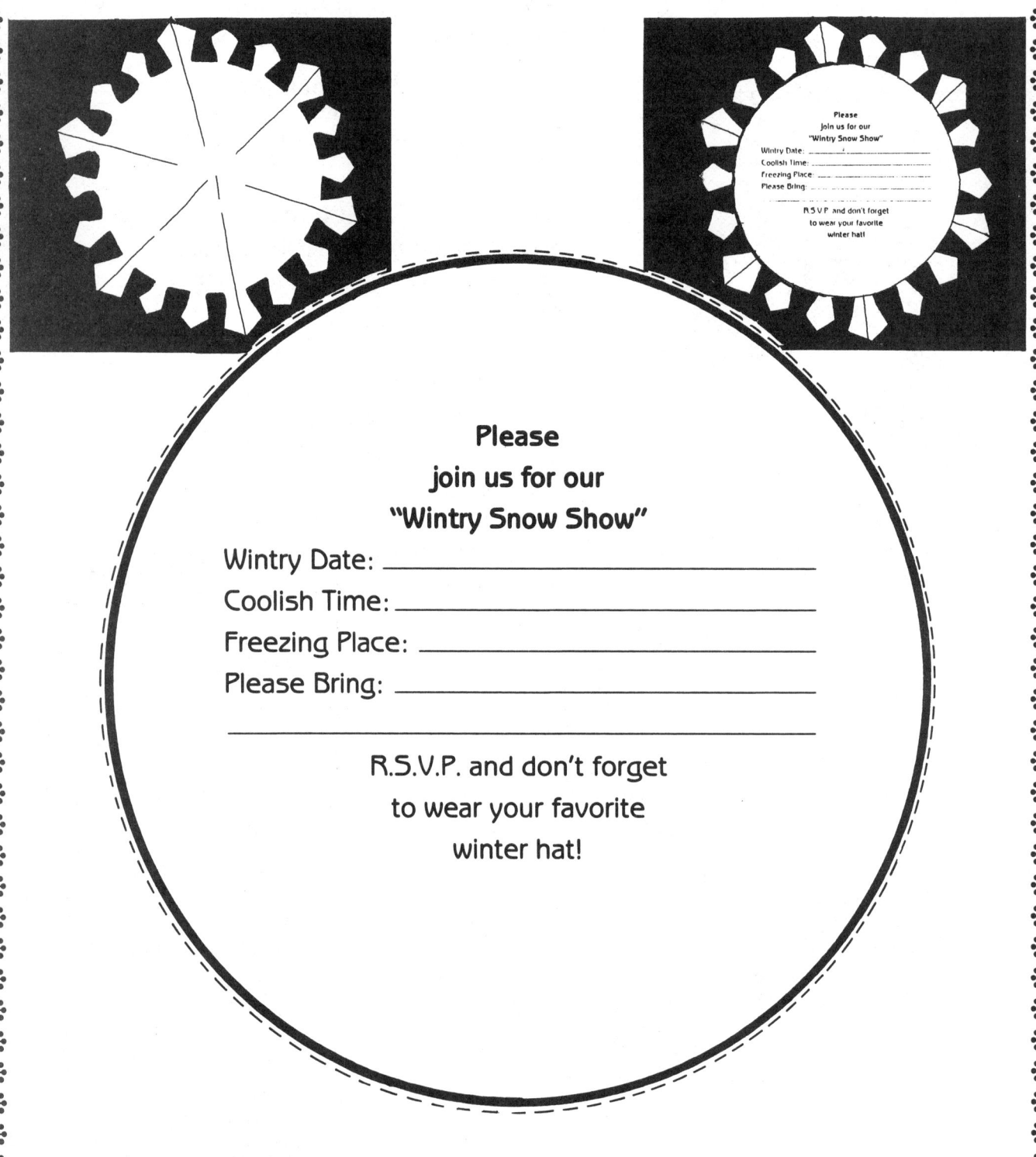

Please
join us for our
"Wintry Snow Show"

Wintry Date: _____

Coolish Time: _____

Freezing Place: _____

Please Bring: _____
_____

R.S.V.P. and don't forget
to wear your favorite
winter hat!

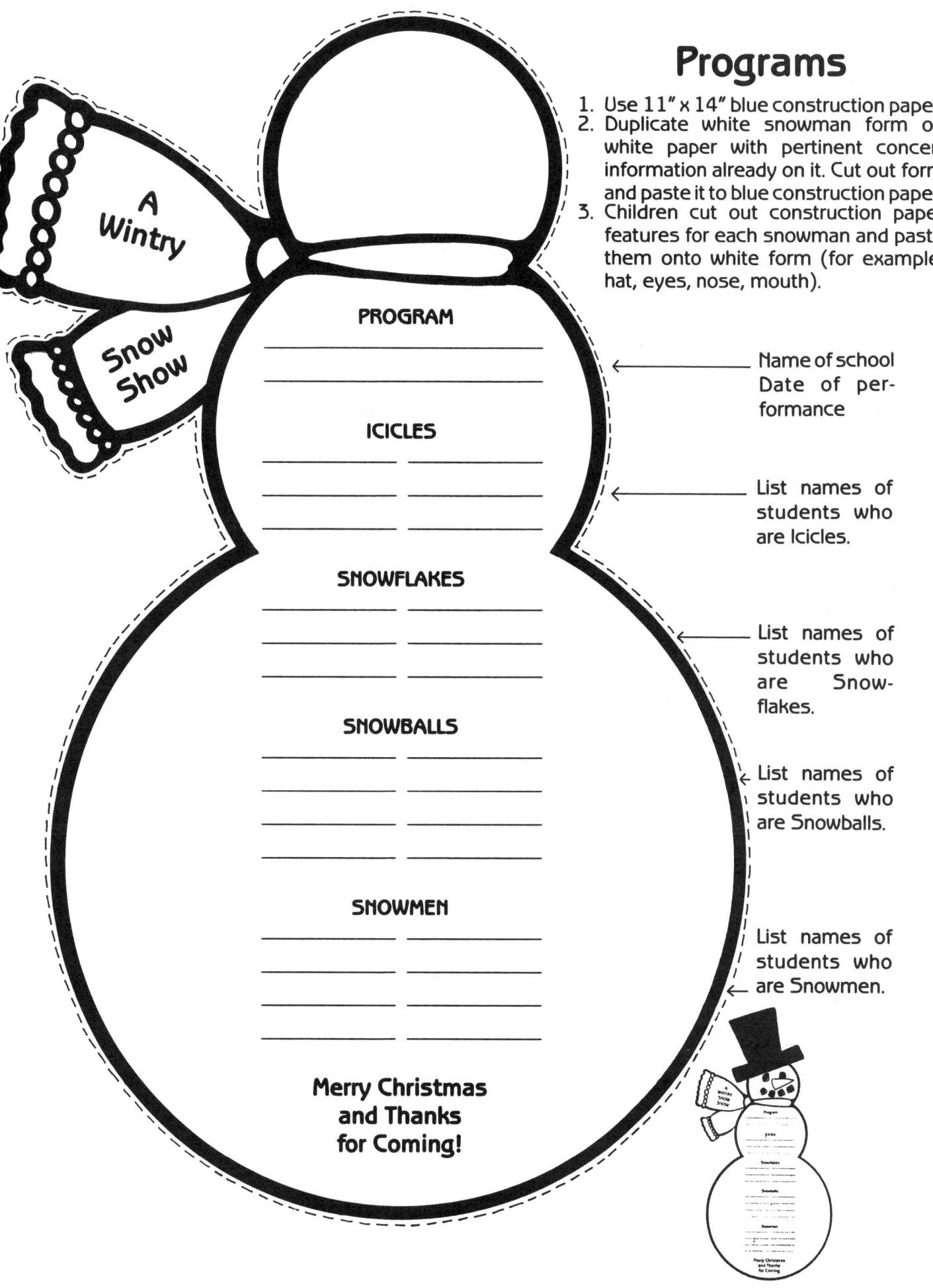

Programs

1. Use 11" x 14" blue construction paper.
2. Duplicate white snowman form on white paper with pertinent concert information already on it. Cut out form and paste it to blue construction paper.
3. Children cut out construction paper features for each snowman and paste them onto white form (for example, hat, eyes, nose, mouth).

← Name of school
   Date of performance

← List names of students who are Icicles.

← List names of students who are Snowflakes.

← List names of students who are Snowballs.

← List names of students who are Snowmen.

Decorations

Name Tags
Parents or invited guests wear name tags corresponding to their child's part in the concert. Teacher duplicates a name tag for each guest.

SNOWMAN

ICICLE

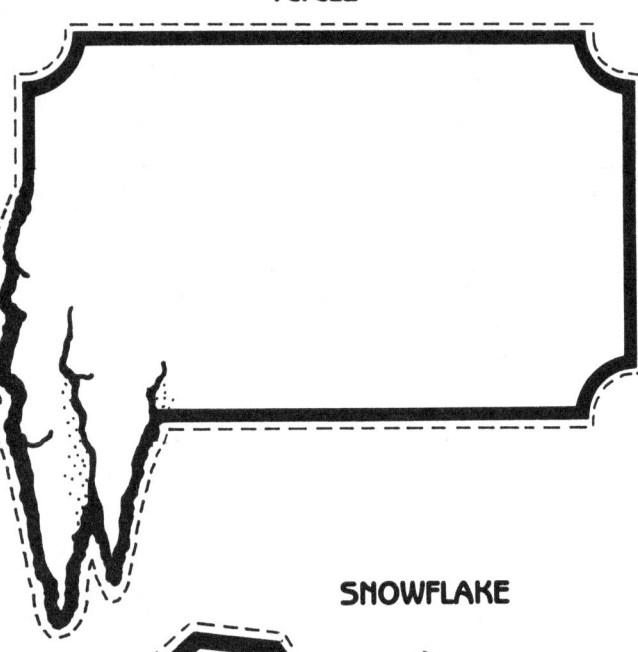

SNOWFLAKE

SNOWBALL

Door Decoration
Make "Br-r-r It's Cold" sign and hang on door.

Br-r-r It's Cold

Room Decorations

1. Students make pastel-colored snowflakes. Hang them from ceiling. (Fold white paper towel. Cut out as you do for a paper snowflake. Dip each end of towel in a different color of diluted food coloring. Unfold and place on newspaper until it dries. When it is dry, staple onto heavy paper circles and hang from ceiling using string.)
2. Put cotton batting in windowsills.
3. Make blue construction paper icicles and hang from the top of each window.
4. Make a bulletin board from children's art to form a snow scene.
5. Decorate a wintry Christmas tree. Obtain a small Christmas tree. Make felt ornaments to represent icicles, snowflakes, snowballs and snowmen. Children paste on bright-colored sequins for added effect. Spray tree with artificial snow. Make a cardboard sign for top of tree in the shape of a snowman. Print *A Wintry Christmas* on the snowman.

Refreshments

Each parent is asked to bring (via the invitation) a refreshment item for after the concert. All refreshments are to be put on a central table for everyone to help themselves.

Chilly Foods and Extras

1. flavored ice cream
2. chocolate syrup topping
3. butterscotch syrup topping
4. marshmallow topping
5. strawberry syrup topping
6. candies (Smarties, Ju-Jubes)
7. candy sprinkles
8. plastic bowls and spoons

Use for make-your-own ice-cream sundaes. With teacher or parent helper supervision, students make sundaes of their choice.

9. vanilla ice cream
10. different varieties of pop
11. plastic cups

Use for make-your-own floats.

12. frozen desserts (for example, yule log)
13. paper plates and forks
14. tea, coffee

For moms, dads and guests.

Additional Chilly Foods

1. ice-cream cones
2. ice-cream waffle sandwiches
3. frozen fruit juice Popsicles
4. round cookies dusted with icing sugar
5. round cookies rolled in coconut
6. cookies cut in the shape of a snowman

Refreshment Table

Cover large table with blue craft mural paper. Trim all edges with cotton batting balls. Make a Santa centerpiece from Styrofoam balls. Make a hat, scarf, eyes, nose and mouth from felt. Make construction paper arms holding a sign "Chilly Foods." (Alternate centerpiece: Hang one snowflake down low from the ceiling. Print "Chilly Foods" on it.)

A Tree-mendous Christmastime

(for one or two grade 2 or grade 3 classes)

"A Tree-mendous Christmastime" is a very simple Christmas concert designed for one or two grade 2 or grade 3 classes. It consists of five songs and one poem to be recited by the whole group. Each student memorizes and sings all five songs and learns the actions to his or her assigned character. This concert can be used in its entirety or can be shortened if necessary. In this concert, students are dressed as Christmas tree adornments. Each group comes forward, sings their song and performs their actions. Then they hang their adornment on the Christmas tree. By the end of the concert the tree is entirely decorated.

The following is a guideline for assigning parts:

Characters	1 Class	2 Classes
Garland	6	12
Ornaments	6	12
Candy Canes	6	12
Stars	6	12

Time Chart

This time chart will allow you to plan in advance the art and music activities required for "A Tree-mendous Christmastime."

Songs and Actions	10 music sessions before concert
Poem Recitation	4 oral reading sessions
Practicing Entire Concert	2 sessions before concert
Dress Rehearsal	morning of concert
Costumes	2 art sessions or have parent helpers make them
Decorations	6 art sessions—display when complete 1 session to color name tags 1 session for popcorn/cranberry hangers 1 session for pinecone hangers 1 session for trees decorated with sequins and glitter 1 session for tissue paper trees 1 session for seed trees
Invitations	10 minutes—send home when complete
Programs	1 art session—delegate one or two students to hand out programs at the door on the day of the concert.
Refreshments	1 session to make tree cookies and Rice Krispie trees 1 session to make candy cane cookies
Concert Setup	On day of concert hang door decoration. Set up benches for children to stand on and chairs for guests to sit on. Set up refreshment table.

Song #1

Our Christmas Tree
(sung to the tune of "Thirty-Two Feet and Eight Little Tails")

Twinkling lights and ornaments and
Pretty red bows and some garland,
All on our Christmas tree,
Decorated up as fine as it can be,
Won't you come and look at it with me?
Rocking horses and some angels,
Reindeer, Santa, bluebirds and bells,
All on our Christmas tree,
Decorated up as fine as it can be,
Won't you come and look at it with me?
Oh, it's wonderful.
Christmas trees are really special and so beautiful.
Lots of tinsel that hangs lightly,
A star on top that shines brightly,
All on our Christmas tree,
Decorated up as fine as it can be,
Won't you come and look at it with me?
It's the best one that you'll ever see.

Staging

Students enter and stand in front of their designated bench. After opening song, Garland take their stage position while all other characters sit down on their bench and sing.

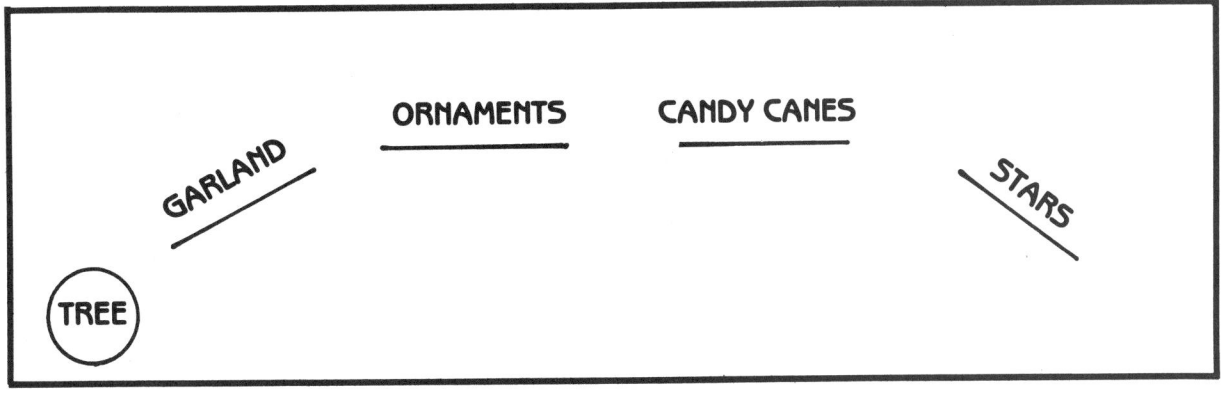

Song #2

Garland
(sung to the tune of "Up on the Housetop")

Some garland will make your tree look bright,
It will sparkle in the light.
Our Christmas tree will look really great,
We're excited, we can hardly wait.
Spark-l-ing, we shine so bright.
Spark-l-ing, we shine so bright.
Some garland will look really great,
Hang us on the tree now, let's not wait.

Actions

Some garland will make our tree look bright,
(march on spot)

It will sparkle in the light.
(sway to right, then to left in time to the music)

Our Christmas tree will look really great,
(march on spot)

We're excited, we can hardly wait.
(point to self with both thumbs, point to audience with right index finger)

Spark-l-ing, we shine so bright.
(turn around) (hands out to side)

Spark-l-ing, we shine so bright.
(turn around) (hands out to side)

Some garland will look really great,
(twirl a piece of garland on costume with right hand)

Hang us on the tree now, let's not wait.
(march on the spot, on the word *us* point to self with both thumbs)

Costumes

Body:
1. Make collar out of heavyweight cardboard.
2. Staple strands of garland onto collar.
3. Tape one piece of garland to front of collar that student can remove to hang on tree.

Head: Pin some garland to hair (i.e., in the form of a headband, around ponytail etc.).

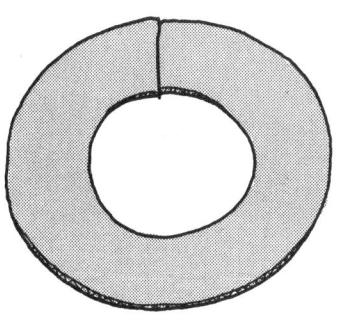

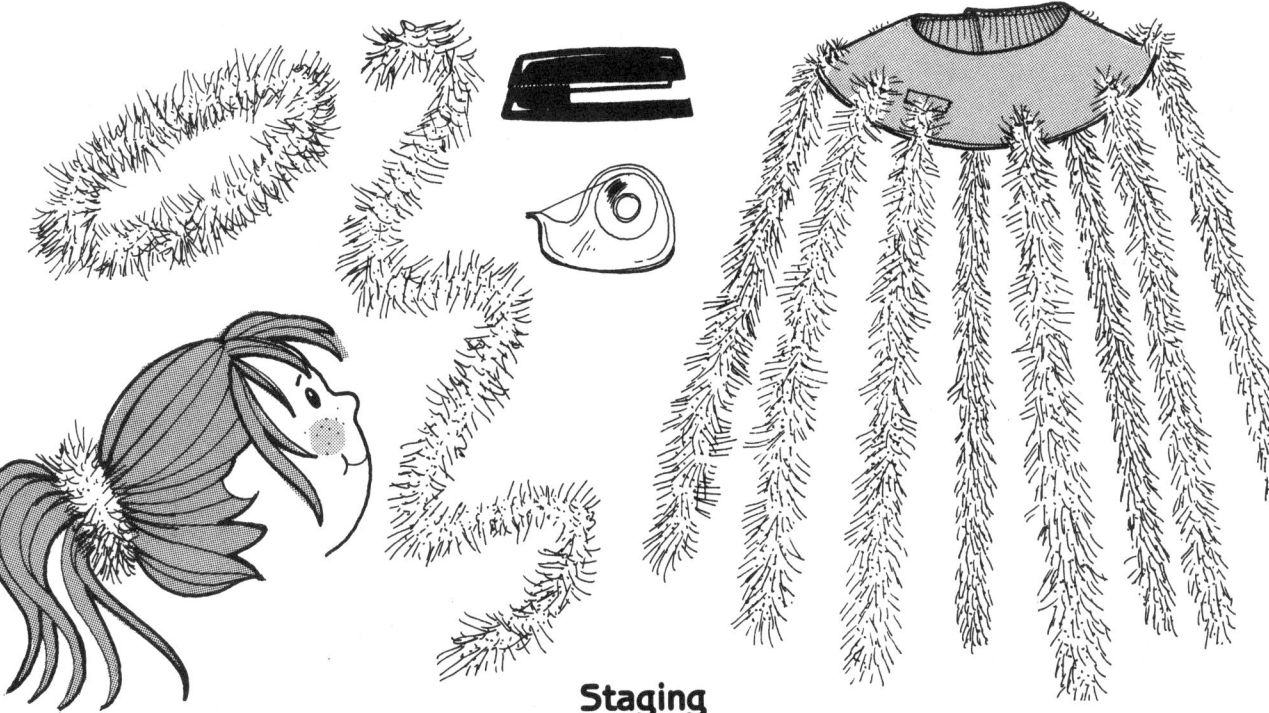

Staging

Before song, Garland leave their bench and take their stage position. After song, Garland march to tree and hang their pieces of garland. They then march to their bench.

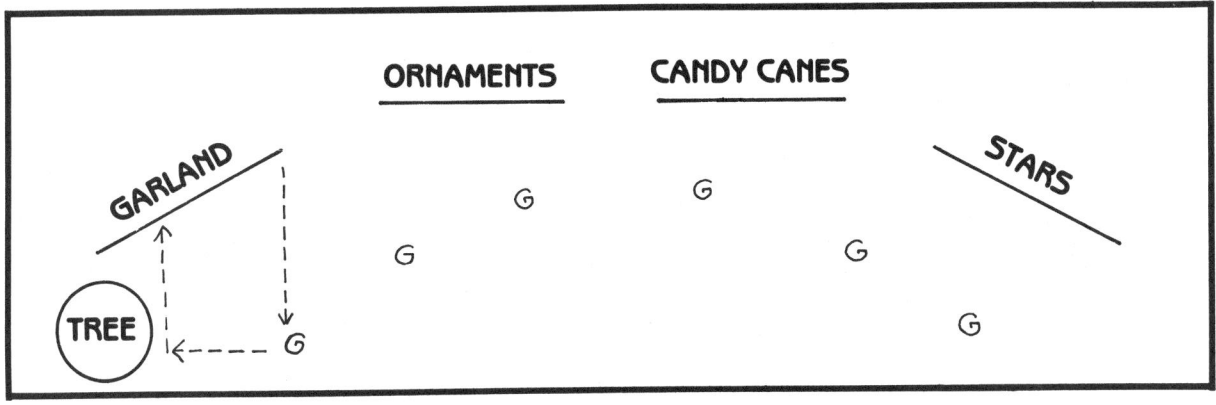

Song #3
Christmas Ornaments
(sung to the tune of "Suzy Snowflake")

Christmas ornaments are what we need on our tree,
Soldiers, reindeer and some little bells
Are just a few you'll see.
Christmas ornaments can make your tree beautiful
Snowflakes, angels and some pretty bows
Are more than suitable.
We all have one special purpose
And that's to help you celebrate
All the happiness that awaits. Oh! This season's great!
Christmas ornaments are what we need on our tree;
We know that it's really going to be such a sight to see.

Actions

Christmas ornaments are what we need on our tree,
(side step to right, snap fingers on right side, side step to left, snap fingers on left side, three times in time to the music, on the word *tree* make an inverted V shape over head with arms)

Soldiers, reindeer and some little bells
(Soldier waves, Reindeer waves, Bell waves)

Are just a few you'll see.
(shake right index finger at audience)

Christmas ornaments can make your tree beautiful
(repeat line 1, on word *beautiful* put hand over heart)

Snowflakes, angels and some pretty bows
(Snowflake waves, Angel waves, Bow waves)

Are more than suitable.
(hands on hips)

We all have one special purpose
(point to self)

And that's to help you celebrate
(shake right index finger at auience)

All the happiness that awaits. Oh! This season's great!
(hands out to side)   (raise right fist in air)

Christmas ornaments are what we need on our tree;
(repeat line 1)

We know that it's really going to be such a sight to see.
(shake right index finger at audience then stretch hands out to audience)

Copyright © 1989, Good Apple, Inc.

Christmas Ornament Costumes

Body:
1. Enlarge drawings of ornaments and trace on heavyweight cardboard. Have students paint, cut out and trim ornaments with garland.
2. Secure large ornaments with string around neck.

Head: Make a hat to go with costume.
Soldier: Make hat out of heavyweight cardboard.
Reindeer: Enlarge pattern on antlers and trace onto heavyweight cardboard. Cut out and attach to headband or hanger bent to fit head.
Bells: Put ribbon in hair.
Snowflake: Put snowflakes in hair. (Cut out paper snowflakes and pin them to hair.)
Angel: Make a wire halo. Cover with garland.
Bows: Put bow in hair.

Ornament: Trace one small ornament for each child. Paint and cut out. Make a tree hanger with ribbon. Tape to chest of costume.

SOLDIERS

REINDEER   BELLS

SNOWFLAKES

ANGELS   BOWS

Staging

Before song, Ornaments leave their bench and take their stage position. After song, Ornaments walk in single file to the tree, take off their small ornaments from their costumes and hang them on the tree. They then return to their bench.

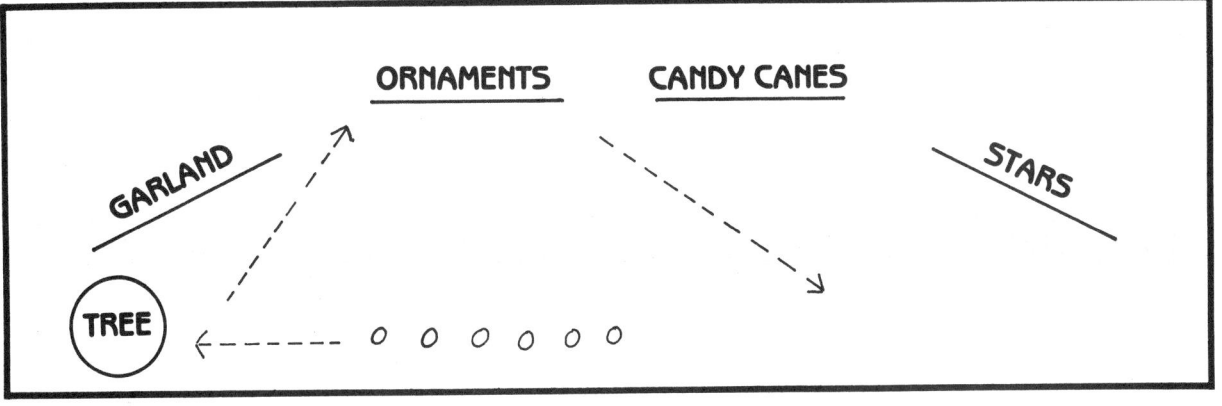

Song #4

Candy Canes
(sung to the tune of "Jingle Bells")

Chorus:
Candy canes, candy canes, candy canes are sweet,
Isn't it so wonderful to have a Christmas tree treat,
Candy canes, candy canes, we're striped red and white,
Hungry kids will think of us as an ornament delight.

Verse:
We hang on the tree, on the branches high and low,
Every place you see, everywhere you go.
We want you to know, happiness and joy,
That we can bring to everyone, especially girls and boys.

Repeat Chorus.

Actions

Candy canes, candy canes, candy canes are sweet,
(move hands like windshield wipers in front of face in time to the music)

Isn't it so wonderful to have a Christmas tree treat,
(repeat line 1) (on the word *treat* raise right fist in air)

Candy canes, candy canes, we're striped red and white,
(repeat line 1)

Hungry kids will think of us as an ornament delight.
(rub belly in circular motion)

We hang on the tree,
(point to self with both thumbs)

On the branches high and low,
(raise hands in air; then lower them to sides, palms out, facing down)

Every place you see, everywhere you go.
(right hand over eyebrows; then point to audience)

We want you to know, happiness and joy,
(point to self with both thumbs; then put hand over heart)

That we can bring to everyone,
(beckon to audience)

Especially girls and boys.
(hands outstretched to side, raise arms in time to the music)

Candy Cane Costumes

Body:
1. Enlarge pattern and trace onto heavyweight cardboard.
2. Paint and cut out candy cane. Trim with garland.
3. Secure to neck with string.

Head:
1. Make headband from construction paper.
2. Trace small candy canes onto lightweight cardboard and paint.
3. Attach candy canes to headband.

Ornament:
1. Cut out small candy cane and paint.
2. Make hanger from ribbon. Tape to chest of costume.

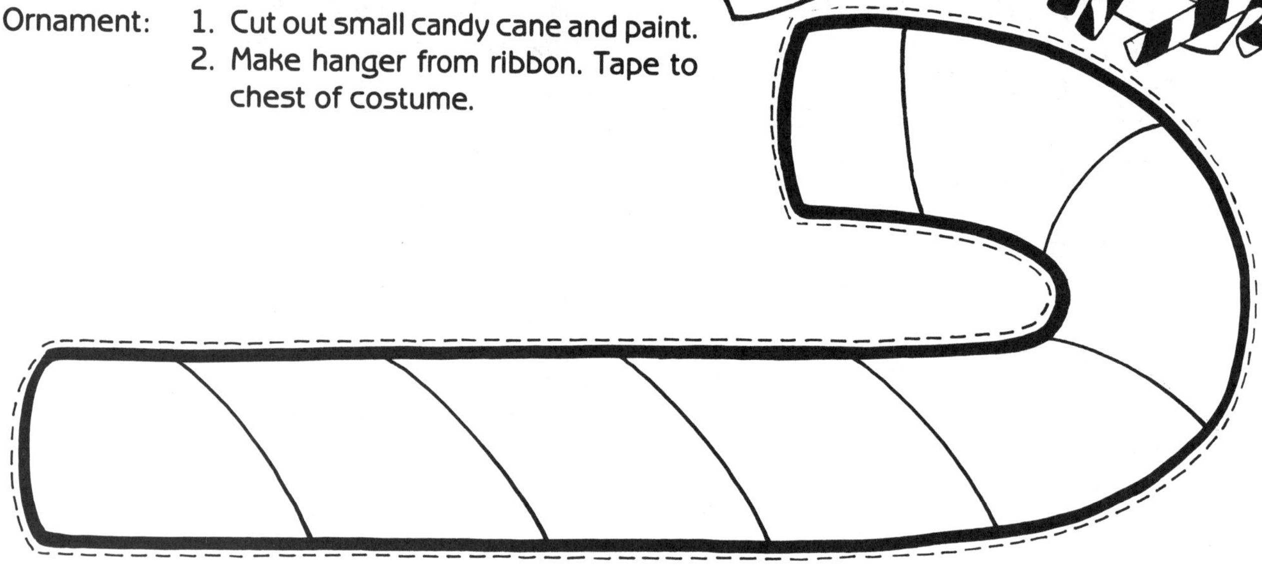

Staging

Before song, Candy Canes come forward and take their stage positions. After song, they walk over to the Chirstmas tree, take off their ornaments, hang them on the tree and return to their bench.

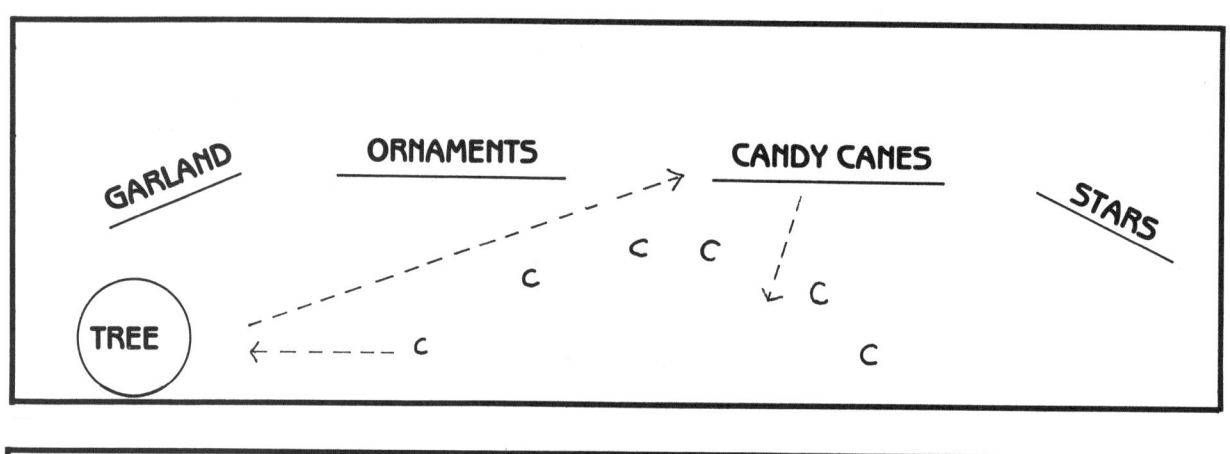

Song #5
Stars
(sung to the tune of "Rudolph the Red-Nosed Reindeer")

Introduction:
We've had soldiers and reindeer and some pretty red bows,
Snowflakes and angels and garland that will glow.
But do you know why we shine brightly i-in the sky?

Verse:
Stars have the place of honor
On top of our Christmas tree.
We will shine down so brightly;
We are such a sight to see.
We can never stop shining
On a tree or in the sky.
We are the ones to guide you,
Now you'll hear the reason why.
We helped the wise men to find
The baby Jesus.
We also guide the reindeer
So that Santa will appear.
Stars have the place of honor
On top of our Christmas tree.
We will shine down so brightly,
We are such a sight to see!

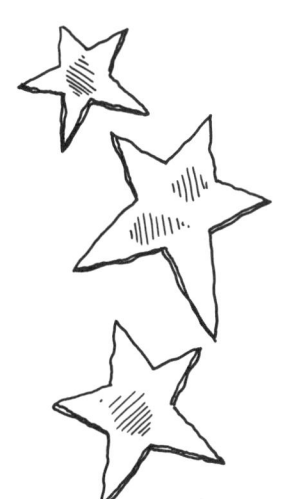

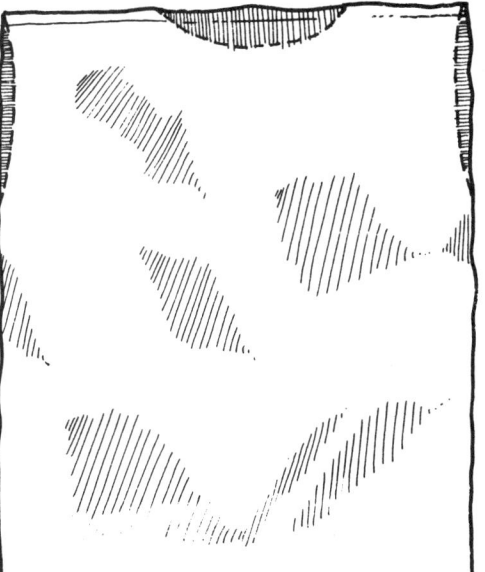

Star Costumes

Body: Cover body with a white garbage bag. Cut holes for neck and arms.

Head:
1. Cut a star shape out of heavyweight cardboard. Cut a circle out of the middle the size of the student's face.
2. Cover star with tinfoil and trim with garland.

Ornament: Cut a small star from lightweight cardboard. Cover it with tinfoil. Tape to garbage bag.

Staging
Before song, Stars come forward and take their stage positions. After song, they walk to Christmas tree, take off their ornaments, hang them on tree and return to their bench.

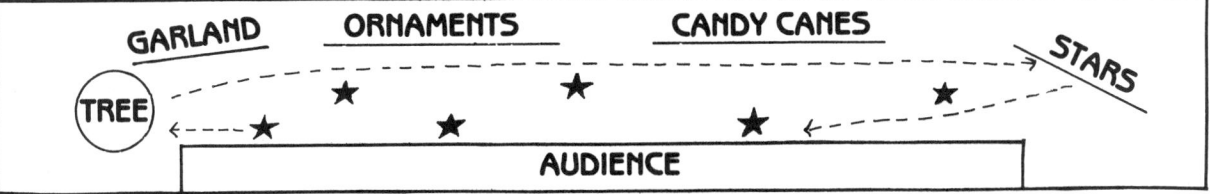

Actions

We've had soldiers and reindeer and some pretty red bows,
(characters on benches wave as their character is called)

Snowflakes and angels and garland that will glow.
(repeat line 1)

But do you know why, we shine brightly i-in the sky?
(shake right index finger at audience; then point to sky)

Stars have the place of honor
(right foot forward, touch heel to floor, point to self with both thumbs)

On top of our Christmas tree.
(make inverted V shape over head with arms)

We will shine down so brightly;
(wave fingers in the air)

We are such a sight to see.
(hands outstretched to side)

We can never stop shining
(wave fingers in air)

On a tree or in the sky.
(make V shape with arms in air; then point to sky)

We are the ones to guide you,
(beckon to audience)

Now you'll hear the reason why.
(shake right index finger at audience)

We helped the wise men to find the baby Jesus.
(put hands over heart; then pretend to rock baby in arms)

We also guide the reindeer so that Santa will appear.
(shake right index finger at audience; then put hands over eyebrows)

Stars have the place of honor
(right foot forward, heel to floor, thumbs point to self)

On top of our Christmas tree.
(make inverted V shape with arms over head)

We will shine down so brightly,
(wave fingers in air)

We are such a sight to see!
(hands outstretched to audience)

Poem
(a choral recitation by all cast members)

(Before poem, all cast members stand in front of their bench to recite poem.)

Our Christmas tree looks just great,
Now we can start to celebrate.
Christmas Day will soon be here;
May your happiness last all year.
Thanks for coming to our play;
We hope you've had a special day.
MERRY CHRISTMAS!

Actions

Our Christmas tree looks just great,
(point to tree)

Now we can start to celebrate.
(fold hands in front of stomach)

Christmas Day will soon be here;
(fold hands in front of stomach)

May your happiness last all year.
(hands outstretched to side)

Thanks for coming to our play;
(hands over heart)

We hope you've had a special day.
(shake right index finger at audience)

MERRY CHRISTMAS!
(wave to audience)

Everyone files off stage.

Invitations

1. Make a copy of invitation for each child.
2. Color lightly.
3. Cut out and mount on red construction paper.
4. Outline star with glitter.

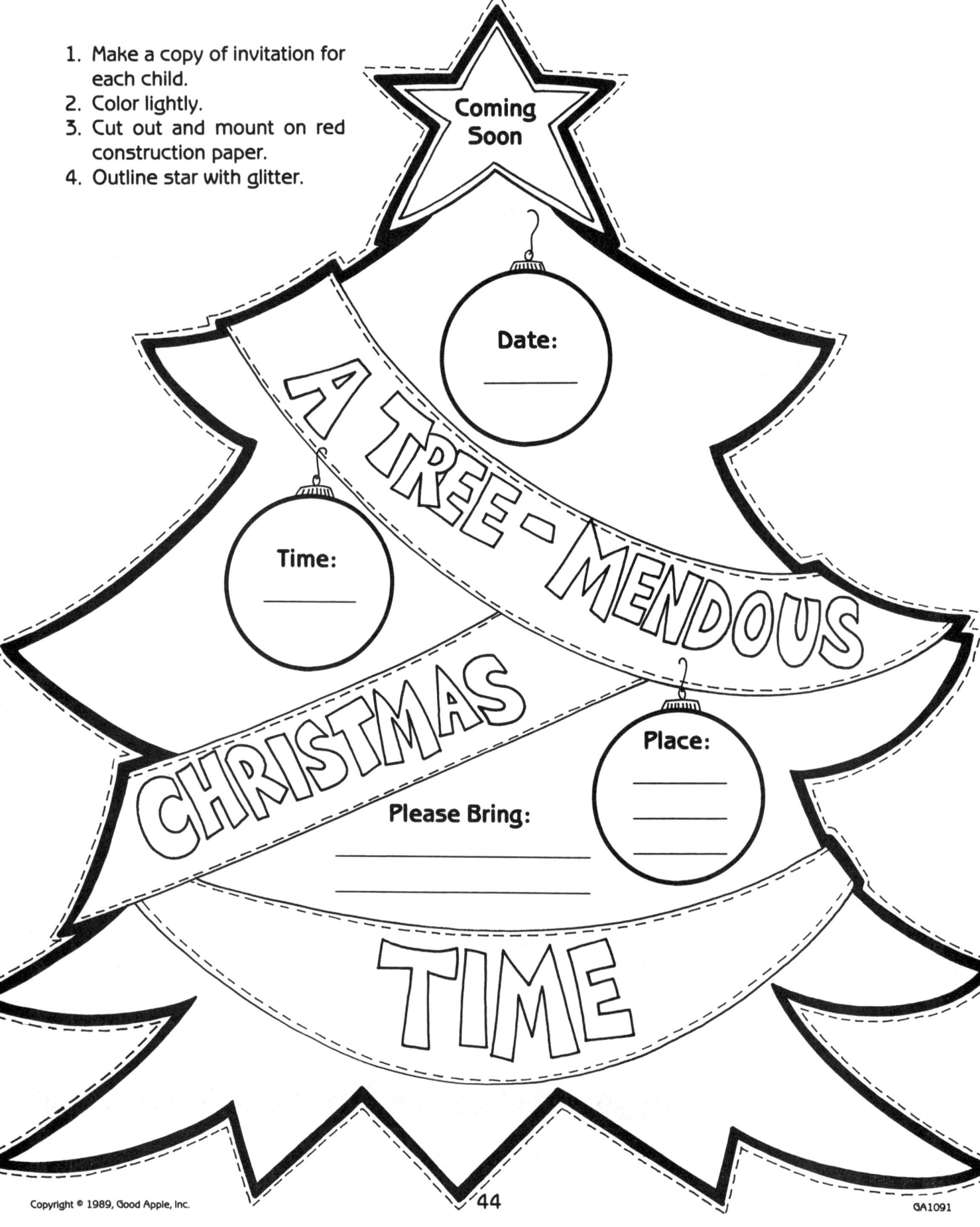

Programs

1. Duplicate large tree form on green construction paper and cut out.
2. Fill in pertinent information on small tree and star and duplicate on white paper. Make one for each program. Cut out.
3. Cut out large star from yellow construction paper. Paste on top of tree.
4. Mount white tree and star on larger tree and star.
5. Fold in half.
6. Decorate outside with student-made paste-on ornaments.

A Tree-mendous Christmas-time

PROGRAM

Date: _____
Place: _____
_____

GARLAND

ORNAMENTS

CANDY CANES

STARS

Names of students who are Garland

Names of students who are Ornaments

Names of students who are Candy Canes

Names of students who are Stars

Decorations

Name Tags
Parents or invited guests wear name tags corresponding to their child's part in the concert. Teacher duplicates a name tag for each guest.

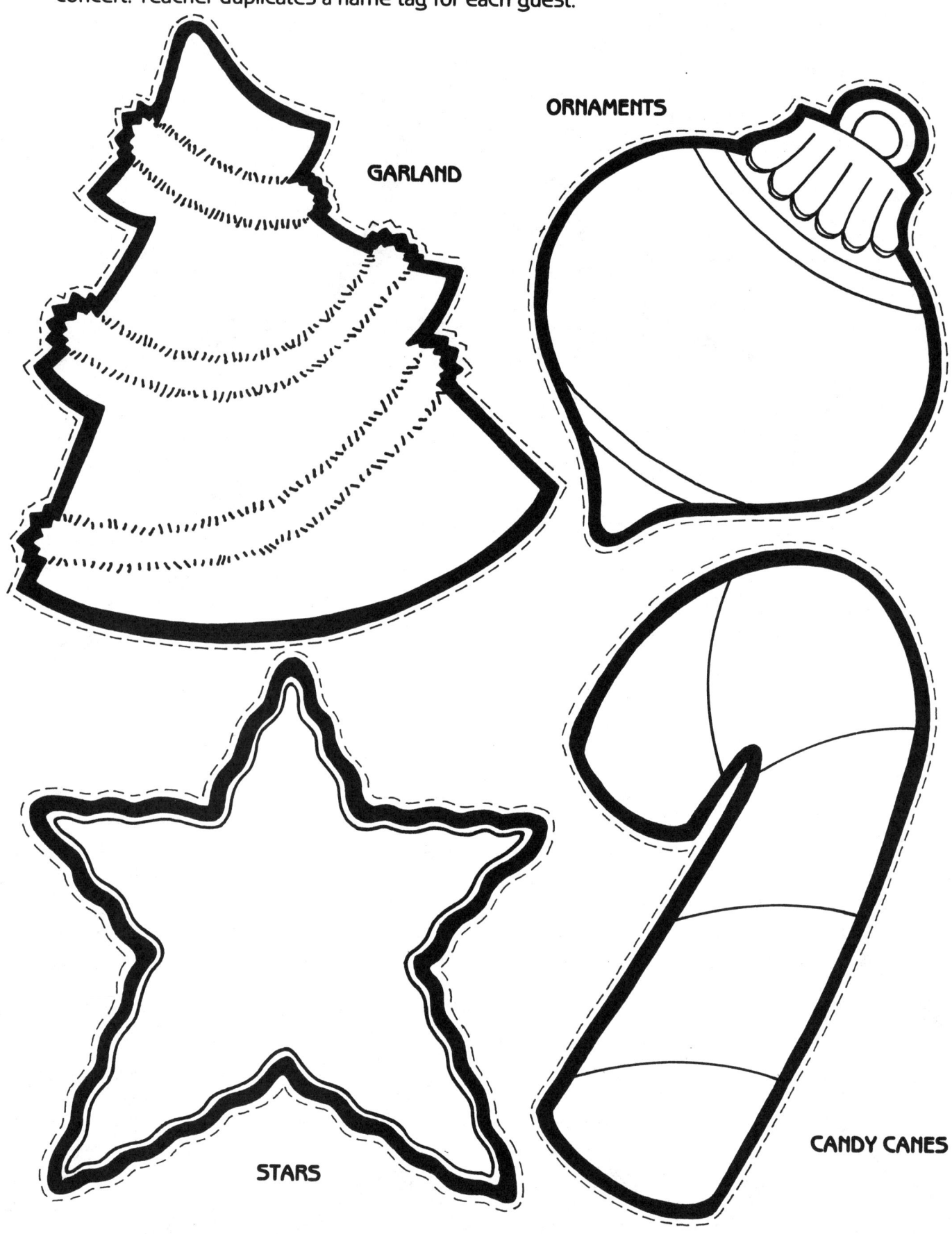

GARLAND

ORNAMENTS

STARS

CANDY CANES

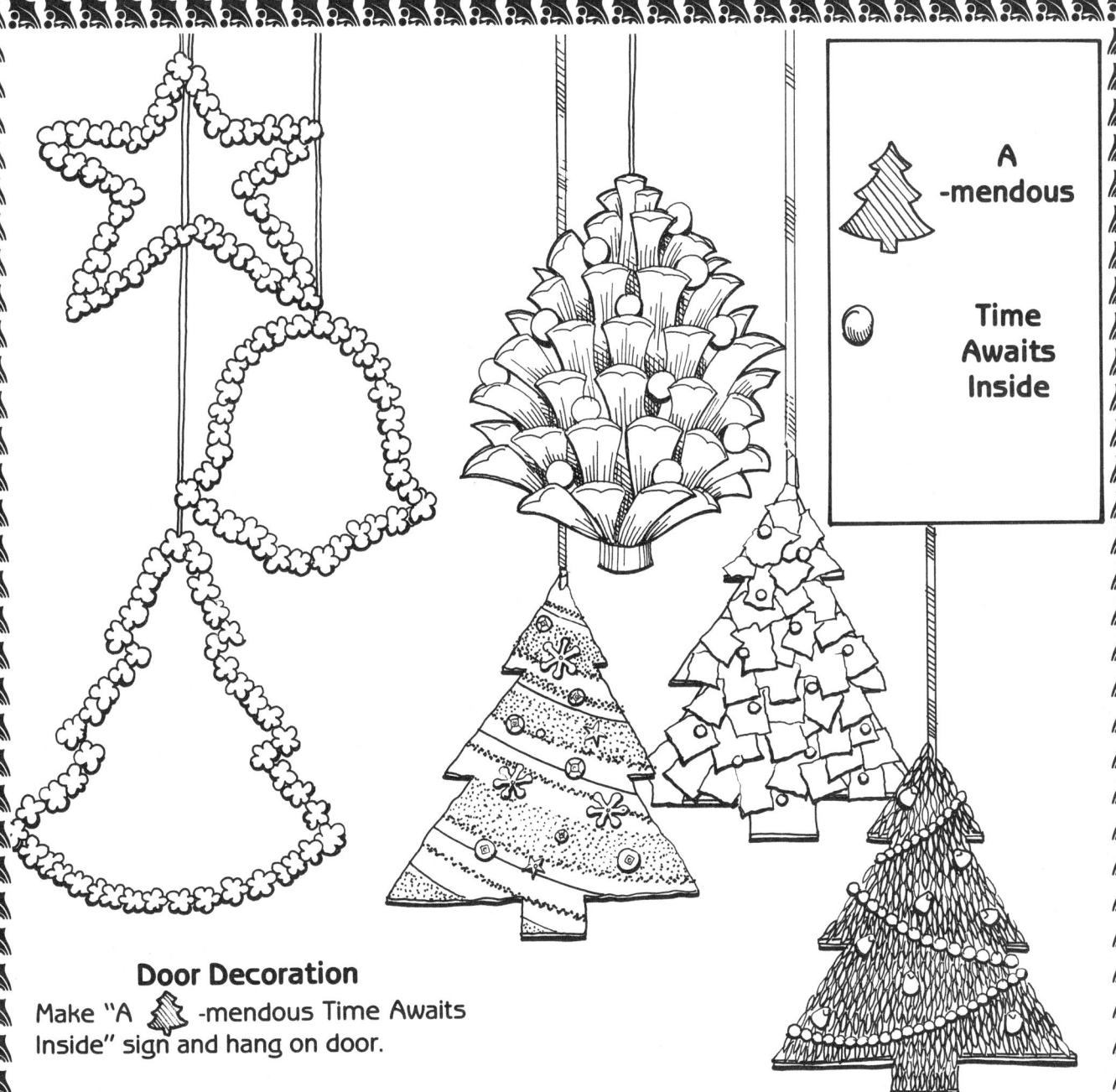

Door Decoration

Make "A 🎄-mendous Time Awaits Inside" sign and hang on door.

Room Decorations

1. String popcorn and/or cranberries on medium weight wire. Shape into stars, bells and trees. Attach strip of ribbon and hang from ceiling.

2. Glue some cedar and some small shiny Christmas balls to the top of large pinecones. Hang from ceiling with ribbon.

3. Create a Christmas tree forest mural. Cut out tree pattern from green construction paper. Decorate with sequins and glitter.

4. Cut out tree shape from lightweight cardboard. Glue on small pieces of tissue paper. Glue on small shiny balls to decorate tree. Add to mural.

5. Cut out tree shape from lightweight cardboard. Glue on a variety of seeds in different patterns to represent ornaments. Display around classroom or add to mural.

Refreshments

Parents are asked to bring (via the invitation) a refreshment item for after the concert. All refreshments are to be put on a central table for everyone to help themselves.

Tree-mendous Treats

1. Make sugar cookies with class. Cut out cookies in the shape of a tree and decorate with green sprinkles. Make a small hole at top of tree. Have parent helper hang cookies with toothpicks (starting from the bottom up) to a Styrofoam cone.

2. Make Rice Krispie squares and have class decorate with M & M's. Cut out in the shape of trees.

3. Make candy cane cookies with class. Prepare shortbread. Color half red. Make strips of each color and twist together.

4. Have two parents make and bring two raw vegetable dishes. Using a 9" x 14" cake pan, build a broccoli tree in the middle. Use cherry tomatoes and radishes for decorations on the tree. Fill in the rest of pan with cauliflower.

5. Have parents bring ham salad, chicken salad and egg salad sandwiches cut in the shape of trees.

6. Have parents bring several different flavors of dip.

7. Serve a lime punch to drink.

Optional: Ice Mold for Punch
Fill Jell-O mold ring with water. Add canned (drained) mandarin orange sections and maraschino cherries to water. Freeze. Unmold and place in punch instead of ice cubes.

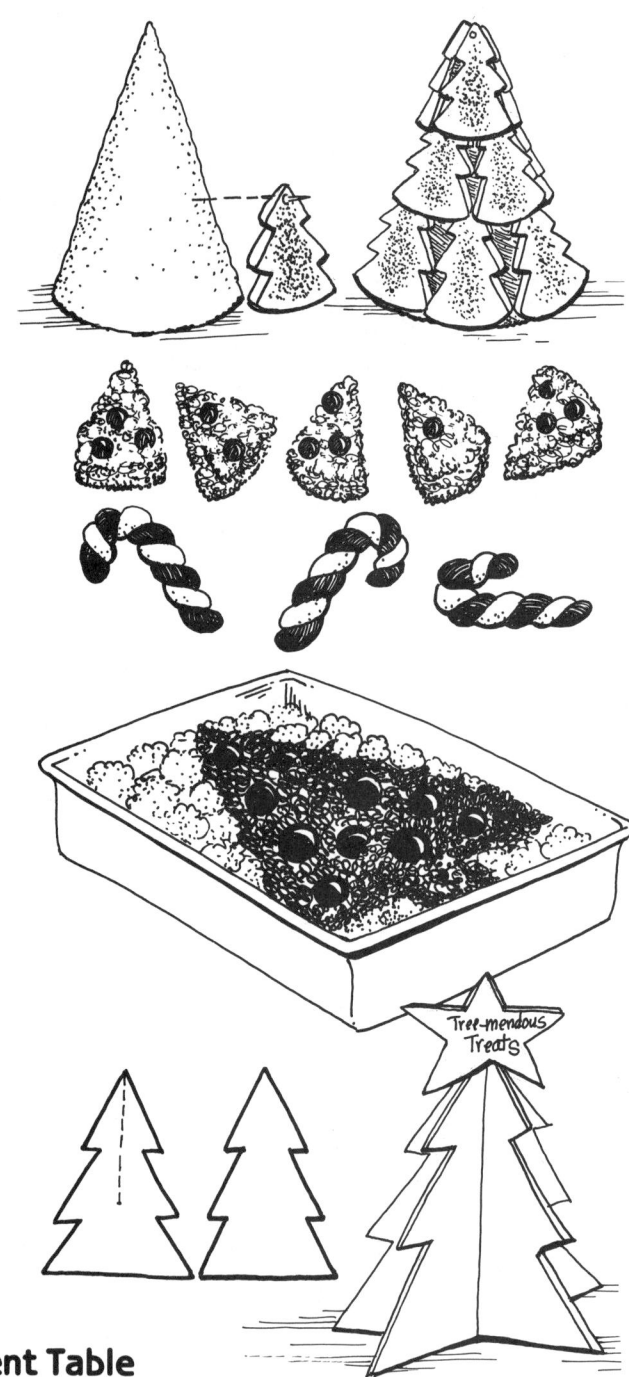

Refreshment Table

Cover table with green mural paper. Decorate with student-made ornaments. Make a tree centerpiece by cutting two identical trees from heavyweight cardboard. Slit one halfway down the middle from the top. Slit the other one halfway up from the bottom. Put together. Attach yellow star on top with "Tree-mendous Treats" on it.

A Fanta-sea Christmas

(for two, three or four primary classes or any primary grouping)

"A Fanta-sea Christmas" takes place under the sea. The sea creatures are hoping Santa will make his first visit to their underwater world this Christmas. They send him a series of notes inviting him to come and meet them. Happy is the underwater world when Santa finally arrives.

This concert is designed for two, three or four primary classes. Any grade from kindergarten to grade three may participate as there are a minimal amount of dialogue, easy songs and simple actions to learn.

The following is a guideline for assigning parts:

Characters	Songs	2 Classes	3 Classes	4 Classes
Santa	"Christmas Under	1	1	1
Reindeer	the Sea"	4	8	8
Octopi	"Ollie and the Gang"	12	18	22
Fishes	"Down in This Ocean"	12	18	22
Shellfish	"Shellfish"	12	18	22
Sea Horses	"Floating thru the Sea"	12	18	22
Everyone	"Christmas Under the Sea"			
	"A Happy, Happy Christmas"			

Concert Songs
Ollie and the Gang
Down in This Ocean
Shellfish
Floating thru the Sea
Christmas Under the Sea
A Happy, Happy Christmas

Music (to the tune of)
"Everett the Evergreen"
"Up on the Housetop"
"Suzy Snowflake"
"Jingle Bells"
"T'was the Night Before Christmas"
"A Holly Jolly Christmas"

Time Chart

This time chart will allow you to plan in advance the art and music activities required for "A Fanta-sea Christmas."

Songs and Actions	10 music sessions before concert
Practicing Entire Concert	4 sessions before concert
Dress Rehearsal	day before concert
Costumes	2 art sessions
Decorations	6 art sessions—display when complete 3 sessions for stuffed fish 3 sessions for fish mural
Invitations	1 art session—send home the same day
Programs	1 art session, 15 minutes—delegate one or two students to hand out programs at the door on the day of the concert.
Refreshments	1 session for fish cookies 1 session for clam chowder
Concert Setup	On day of concert hang door decoration. Set up refreshment table. Set up chairs for audience as well as staging props.

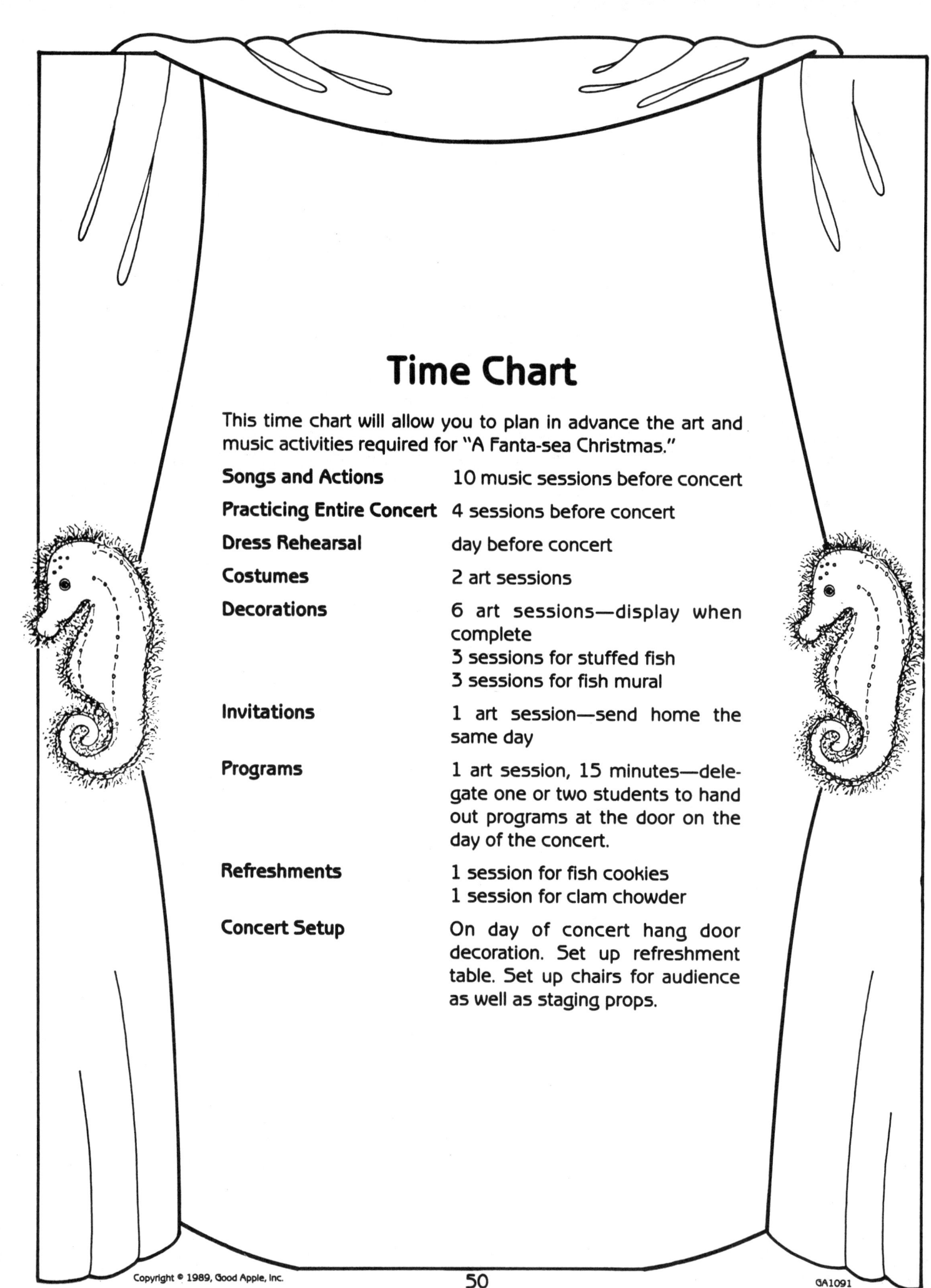

A Fanta-sea Christmas

At the beginning of the concert, the stage is empty, with Sign #1 at the far right.

Enter Octopi and take their places on stage in a semicircle formation, facing the audience. Center Octopus has a banner with *Ollie* printed on it attached to his costume. He also carries a large note to Santa which he puts on the floor facedown in front of him.

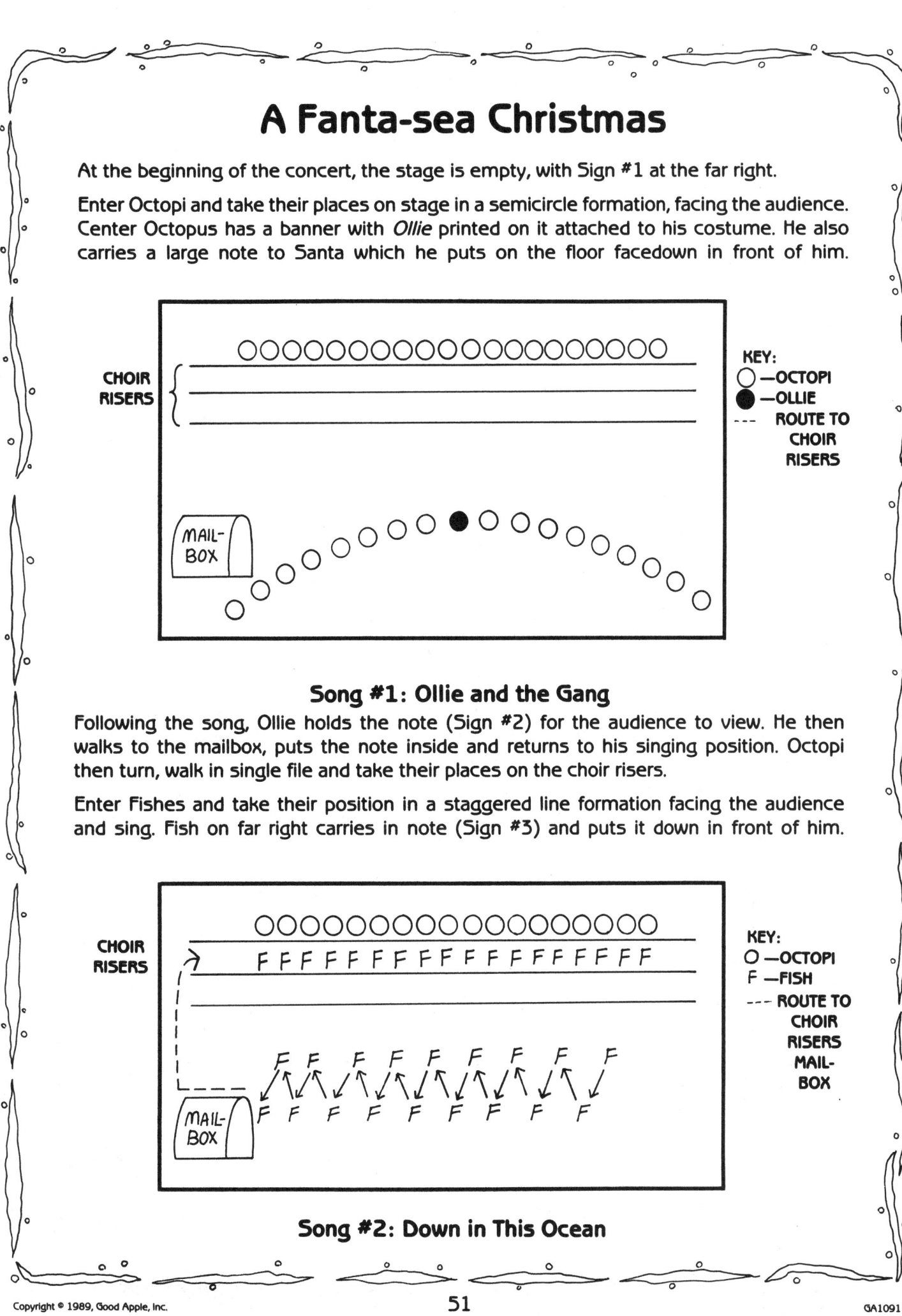

Song #1: Ollie and the Gang

Following the song, Ollie holds the note (Sign #2) for the audience to view. He then walks to the mailbox, puts the note inside and returns to his singing position. Octopi then turn, walk in single file and take their places on the choir risers.

Enter Fishes and take their position in a staggered line formation facing the audience and sing. Fish on far right carries in note (Sign #3) and puts it down in front of him.

Song #2: Down in This Ocean

At the end of the song, Fish on the far right holds up Sign #3 for the audience to view. He then takes the note over to the mailbox, puts it in and returns to his position. Fishes then turn and take their places on the middle row of the choir risers.

Enter Shellfish and take their positions on stage in a straight line formation facing the audience. Shellfish on far right carries in note (Sign #4) and puts it facedown on the floor in front of him.

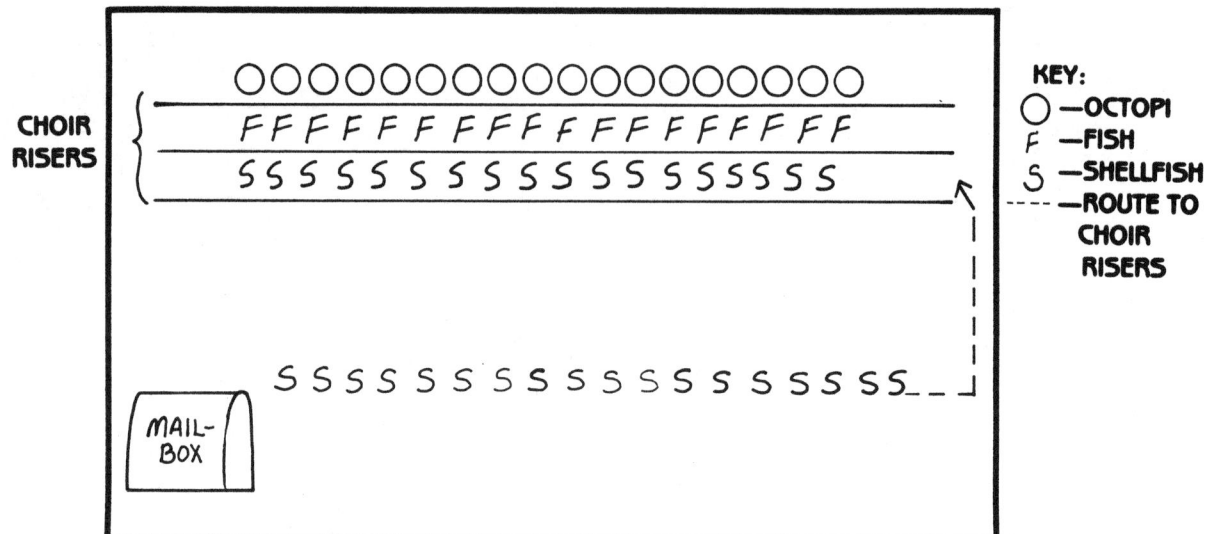

Song #3: Shellfish

At the end of the song, the Shellfish on the far right holds up Sign #4 for the audience to view. He carries it over to the mailbox, puts it in and returns to his position. All the Shellfish turn and take their places on the bottom row of the choir risers.

Enter Sea Horses and take straight line position kneeling at the edge of the stage with tails hanging over the edge so they are able to sway as song is being sung. Sea Horse on the far right carries Sign #5 and puts it down behind him.

Song #4: Floating thru the Sea

At the end of the song, Sea Horse at the far right holds up Sign #5 for the audience to view, puts it in the mailbox and returns to singing position. Sea Horses stay in kneeling position for the duration of the concert.

Enter Submarine being pulled through the audience by Reindeer. All children on stage sing.

Song #5: Christmas Under the Sea

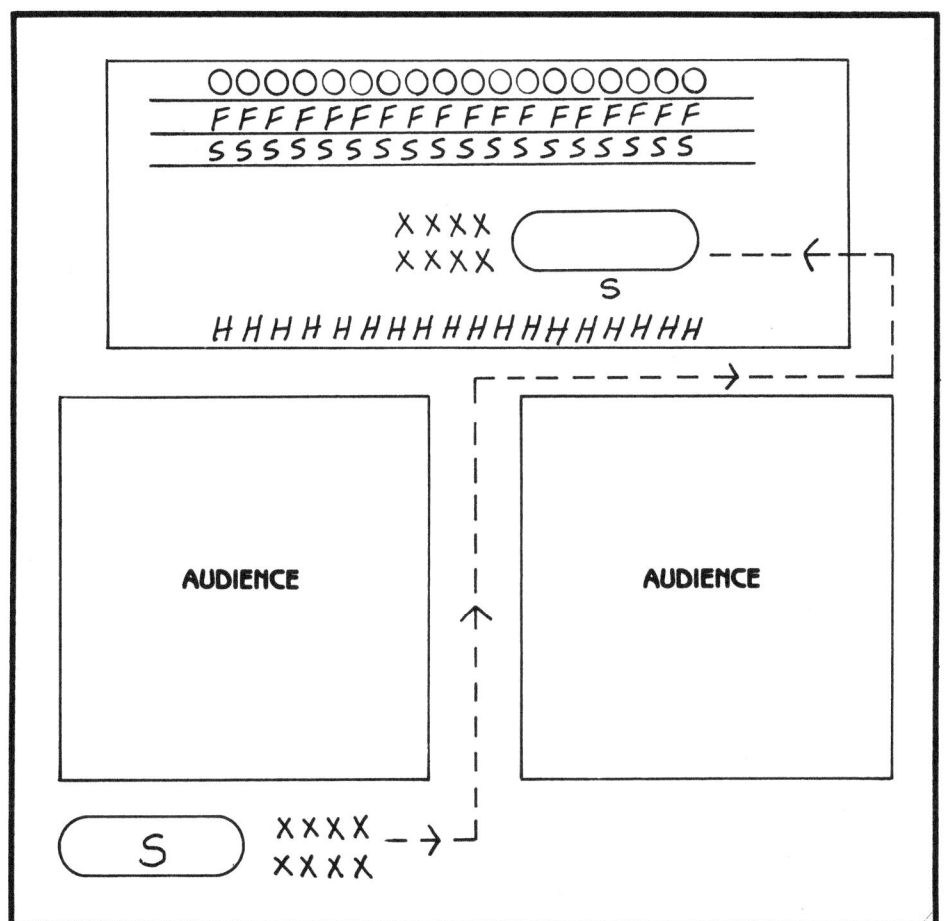

At end of song, Santa, followed by Reindeer, take their places on center stage. Santa says:

"Ho! Ho! Ho! What a wonderful place you have down here. When I received all your delightful notes, I knew I had to come down for a visit to thank you for your very kind invitations. Have a very Merry Christmas one and all! Ho! Ho! Ho!"

Song #6: A Happy, Happy Christmas

During song Santa holds up Sign #6.

After song, everyone files off stage.

Song #1
Ollie and the Gang
(sung to the tune of "Everett the Evergreen")

Ollie the octopus
And all the rest of us
Are gathered together today.
Santa Claus has never been here;
We want him to visit this year.
We will send him a note this way.
To all us octopi,
He is our fav-rite guy.
We need this jolly man right here.
So here's our note to invite him,
Wouldn't it be great to meet him
And all of his funny reindeer.
So with this note
Be sure to come and visit each of us;
You could make our Christmas
The best it could ever be.
You don't have to bring us presents
Or even start to fuss.
It's lots of fun down here
You are bound to see.
Ollie the octopus
And all the rest of us
Invite you down under the sea.
Come and join our festivities,
Happy and fun activities,
Our Christmas will be great indeed!

Octopi Costumes

Head:
1. Cut round circle out of orange or purple cardboard.
2. Cut hole for head.
3. Attach string at either side to attach to head.

Tentacles: From shoulder, pin on purple or orange crepe paper to represent tentacles. Alternate these strips with garland.

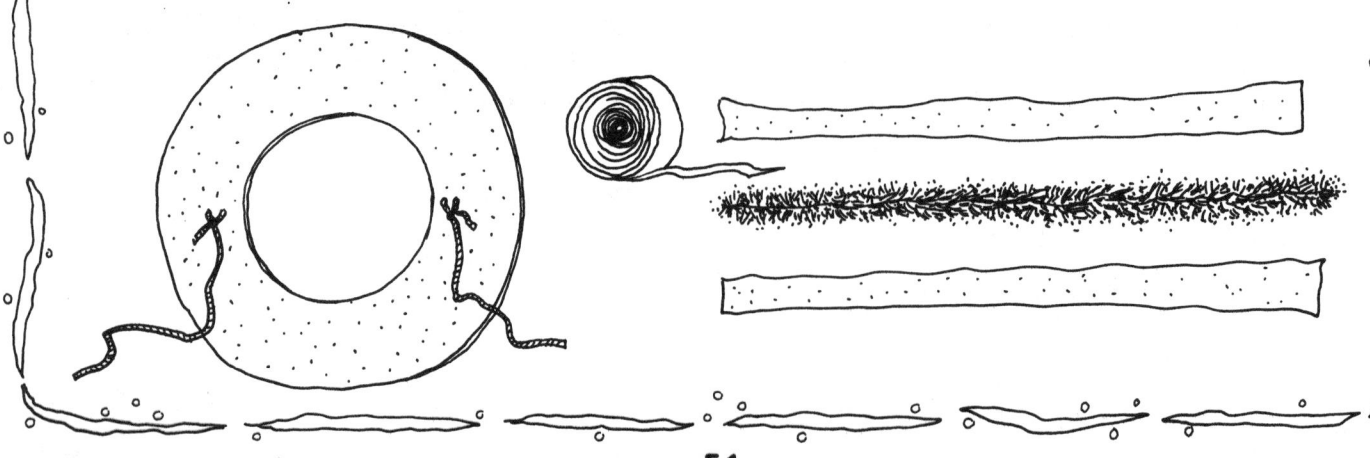

Actions

Ollie the octopus and all of the rest of us
(point to audience)   (point to self)

Are gathered here today. Santa Claus has never been here;
(hands out to side; then hands in front making Santa's belly)

We want him to visit this year.
(beckon to audience)

We will send him a note this way.
(point to mailbox)

To all us octopi, he is our fav-rite guy.
(left hand on hip, shake right index finger at audience)

We need this jolly man right here.
(hands out to side)

So here's our note to invite him,
(Ollie holds up note)

Wouldn't it be great to meet him and all of his funny reindeer.
(clasp hands and hold under chin; then put hands on top of head to represent antlers)

So with this note be sure to come and visit each of us;
(Ollie holds up note; then all beckon to audience; then point to each other)

You could make our Christmas the best it could ever be.
(shake finger at audience; then put hands out to side)

You don't have to bring us presents
(shake head in disagreement)

Or even start to fuss.
(hands on hips)

It's lots of fun down here you are bound to see.
(both index fingers point down; then point to audience)

Ollie the octopus and all the rest of us
(point to Ollie, then to self)

Invite you down under the sea.
(left hand on hip, point down with right index finger)

Come and join our festivities, happy and fun activities,
(beckon to audience; then trace smile on face with finger)

Our Christmas will be great indeed!
(hands out to side)

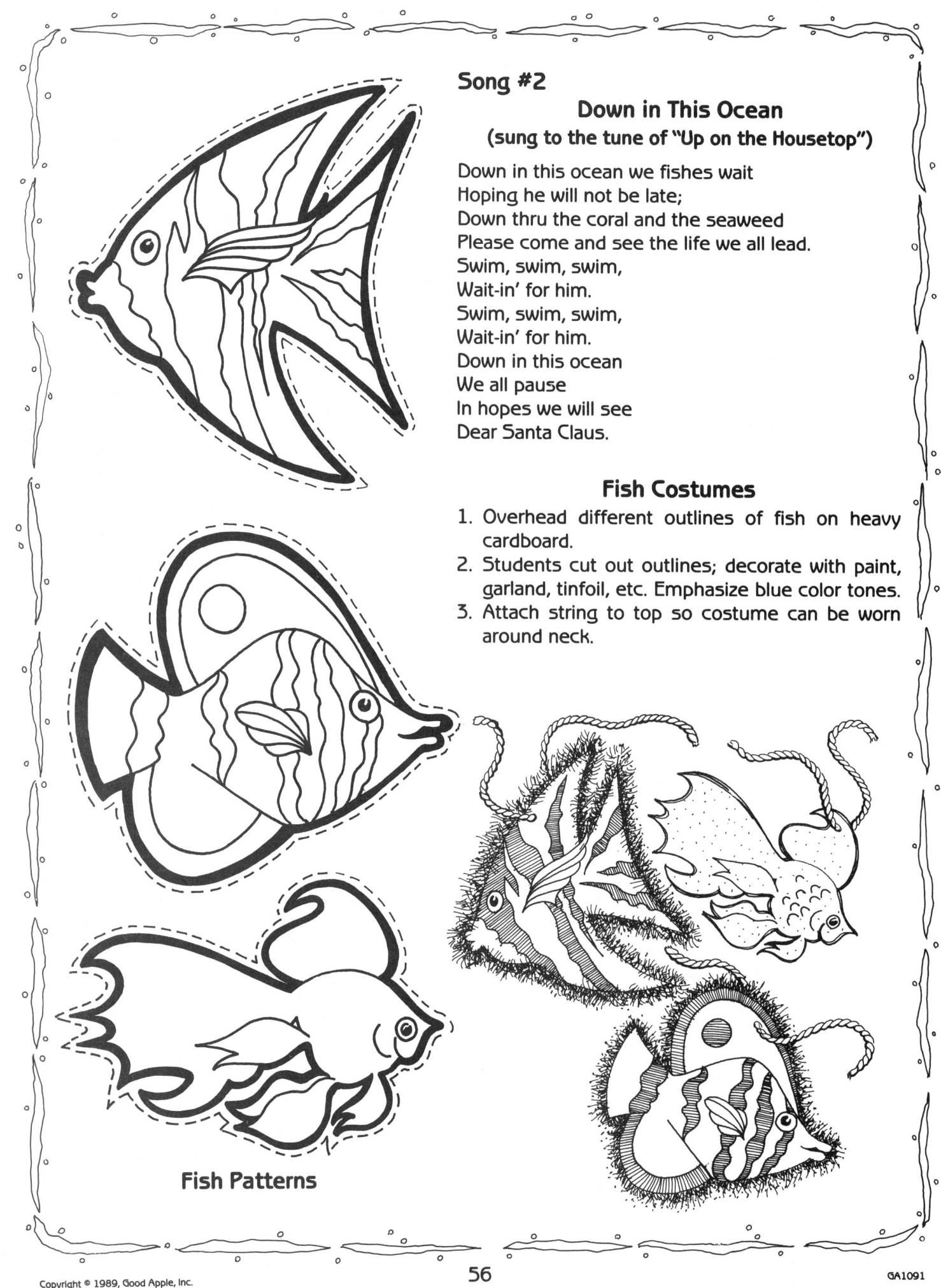

Song #2

Down in This Ocean
(sung to the tune of "Up on the Housetop")

Down in this ocean we fishes wait
Hoping he will not be late;
Down thru the coral and the seaweed
Please come and see the life we all lead.
Swim, swim, swim,
Wait-in' for him.
Swim, swim, swim,
Wait-in' for him.
Down in this ocean
We all pause
In hopes we will see
Dear Santa Claus.

Fish Costumes

1. Overhead different outlines of fish on heavy cardboard.
2. Students cut out outlines; decorate with paint, garland, tinfoil, etc. Emphasize blue color tones.
3. Attach string to top so costume can be worn around neck.

Fish Patterns

Actions

Down in this ocean we fishes wait
(sway to right then to left in time to the music)

Hoping he will not be late;
(keep swaying)

Down thru the coral and the seaweed
(keep swaying)

Please come and see the life we all lead.
(keep swaying)

Swim, swim, swim,
(pretend to breaststroke)

Wait-in' for him.
(hands on hips)

Swim, swim, swim,
(pretend to breaststroke)

Wait-in' for him.
(hands on hips)

Down in this ocean
(squat down)

In hopes we will see
(stand up, put hands over eyes)

Dear Santa Claus.
(make Santa's belly with arms in front of stomach)

Song #3
Shellfish
(sung to the tune of "Suzy Snowflake")

Here come all the shellfish
Right on the ocean floor
Write, write, writing a note to Santa;
They'd like to see him more.
Here come all the shellfish
They want to celebrate;
Christmas is the only time of year,
So let's make it real great.
If you wanna see a lobster,
We've got a lot that you can meet.
If you wanna see an oyster,
Here are some to greet.
Crabs, clams and some starfish, too,
Want Santa to come here,
Bringing happiness and lots of joy
At this time of year.

Shellfish Costumes

1. Overhead different outlines of clams, oysters, starfish, crabs and lobsters on heavy cardboard. Cut hole for head.

2. Students cut out outlines and decorate with paint and garland. Emphasize red and orange tones.

3. Attach string to sides to keep mask on head.

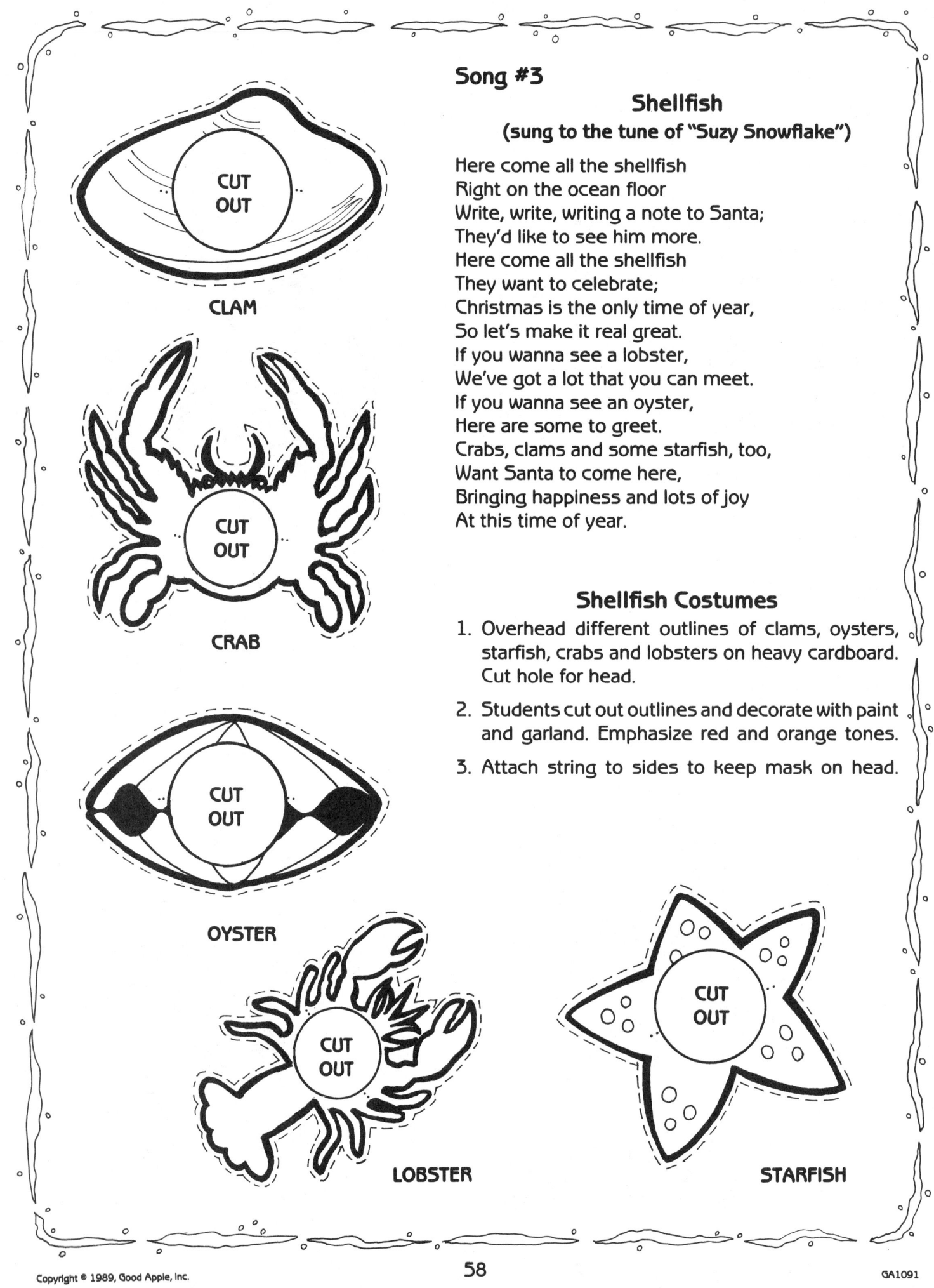

CLAM

CRAB

OYSTER

LOBSTER

STARFISH

Actions

Here come all the shellfish
(walk on spot)

Right on the ocean floor
(walk on the spot)

Write, write, writing a note to Santa;
(left hand out, pretend to write on it with right hand)

They'd like to see him more.
(hands on hips)

Here come all the shellfish
(walk on spot)

They want to celebrate;
(walk on spot)

Christmas is the only time of year,
(hands out to side, raising them in time to the music)

So let's make it real great.
(keep raising hands in time to the music)

If you wanna see a lobster,
(Lobsters take one step out)

We've got a lot that you can meet.
(Lobsters wave to audience then step back)

If you wanna see an oyster,
(Oysters take one step forward)

Here are some to greet.
(Oysters wave; then step back)

Crabs, clams, some starfish, too,
(Crabs, Clams, Starfish step forward)

Want Santa to come here,
(Crabs, Clams, Starfish wave; then step back)

Bringing happiness and lots of joy
(hands out to side)

At this time of year.
(raise hands in time to the music)

Song #4
Floating thru the Sea
(sung to the tune of "Jingle Bells")

Floating thru the sea
Greeting lots of fish we know
Happy as can be
Santa's sure to come.
Once he reads our note
He'll want to join in all the fun;
Maybe he'll come by boat.

Chorus:
Sea horses, sea horses,
Floating thru the sea,
Oh what fun we'll have
With Santa it will surely be.
Sea horses, sea horses,
Floating thru the sea
Oh what fun we'll have
With Santa it will surely be.

Sea Horse Costumes
1. Overhead outline of sea horses on large pieces of heavy cardboard.
2. Students paint them lemon yellow and lime green. Trim with garland.
3. Hang costume from neck with string.

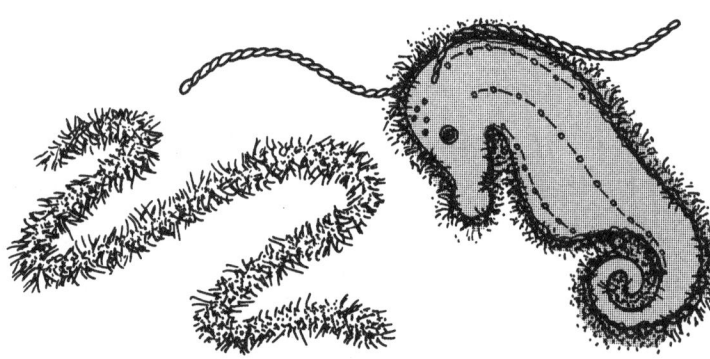

Actions
Sea Horses come on stage and kneel at the edge of the stage. They put their tails over the edge and move their costumes in time to the music to create swaying motion.

Song #5

Christmas Under the Sea
(sung to the tune of "T'was the Night Before Christmas")

Sing twice.

It's the night before Christmas and under the sea
All the fishes are working as hard as can be.
The coral is gleaming and the seaweed is hung,
Our playground is ready for Santa to come.
Old King Neptune says Santa can't even swim;
His reindeer need air so they can't come with him.
We won't have a Christmas is wha-at we fear;
We won't get to see all his funny reindeer,
But the magic mermaid says he'll think of a way
To come under the ocean on this special day.
And so all of the oysters and all of the clams,
All of the sea horses have made so many plans.
They want to see Rudolph and that jolly fat man;
They have done ev-er-ything that they possibly can.
Then what to their wand'ring eyes should appear
A submarine ship containing reindeer;
The jolly old driver is dressed all in gear—
This is def-in-ite-ly the best time of year.
Santa and his reindeer have come to celebrate;
What a Christmas Day we will have
Just you-ou wait!

Santa and Reindeer Costumes

Santa: Wear red track suit. Use scuba diving equipment.

Alternative:
Head: Papier-mâché a large round balloon. When dry, cut holes for eyes. Paint.

Air Tanks: Papier-mâché two oblong balloons. Paint black and attach to back. Attach vacuum cleaner hose to headpiece and air tanks.

Reindeer: Dress in brown.

Antlers: Outline two antlers on cardboard for each child. Have each child cover antlers with tinfoil. Attach antlers to a headband or a coat hanger bent to fit the head of the child.

SANTA AND SCUBA GEAR

ANTLERS

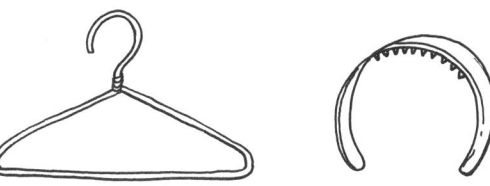

Actions

It's the night before Christmas and under the sea
(scooping action downward with right hand)

All the fishes are working as hard as can be.
(breaststroke quickly)

The coral is gleaming and the seaweed is hung,
(put hands over eyes then pretend to hang seaweed)

Our playground is ready for Santa to come.
(both hands out to audience)

Old King Neptune says Santa can't even swim;
(shake head back and forth in disagreement)

His reindeer need air so they can't come with him.
(put hands over head to represent antlers)

We won't have a Christmas is wha-at we fear;
(shake head back and forth, point finger back and forth)

We won't get to see all his funny reindeer,
(put hands on head to represent antlers)

But the magic mermaid says he'll think of a way
(put finger to head as in thinking action)

To come under the ocean on this special day.
(repeat line 1)

And so all of the oysters and all of the clams,
(Oysters and Clams wave)

All of the sea horses have made so many plans.
(Sea Horses wave)

They want to see Rudolph and that jolly fat man;
(put thumb and forefinger together on both hands)

They have done ev-er-ything that they possibly can.
(put both hands up to eyes to represent binoculars)

Then what to their wand'ring eyes should appear
(put hand over eyes)

A submarine ship containing reindeer;
(point to submarine coming up aisle)

The jolly old driver is dressed all in gear—
(point to Santa)

This is def-in-ite-ly the best time of year.
(hands on hips)

Santa and his reindeer have come to celebrate;
(shake finger at audience)

What a Christmas Day we will have just you-ou wait!
(shake finger at audience; then point to self; then put hands out to side)

Song #6
A Happy, Happy Christmas
(sung to the tune of "A Holly Jolly Christmas")

It's a happy, happy Christmas
Now that Santa has come here;
We all know he's wonderful
And so are his reindeer.
It's a happy, happy Christmas
And way down in the sea,
We will have a super time
As sure as you can be.
Dive went the submarine
To the ocean floor;
Now we're much happier
Then we've been before.
It's a happy, happy Christmas
We are sure you will agree;
It will be a very happy Christmas
Under the sea!

Copyright © 1989, Good Apple, Inc.

Props

Mailbox
1. Paint a tall cardboard box red.
2. Label in large letters *Underwater Mailbox*.

Submarine
1. Overhead onto large pieces of corrugated cardboard two sides of a submarine.
2. Paint it grey.
3. Cut out.
4. Attach the sides to a gym equipment box (must have wheels).
5. Trim with garland.
6. Attach rope to the front end so reindeer can pull it.

Signs

Sign #1

Date:
December 19--

Place:
Ocean Deep

Sign #2

Dearest Santa,
Please visit us
on Christmas Day.
Love,
Ollie and the Gang

Sign #3

Dear Mr. Claus,
We really hope
to see you soon.
Best regards,
The Fishes

Sign #4

To Rudolph,
Please ask Santa
to come and visit us.
Sincerely,
The Shellfish

Sign #5

Dear Mrs. Claus,
Please make sure
your husband drops
down at Christmas.
Yours truly,
The Sea Horses

Sign #6

Merry Christmas
from under the
sea!

Invitations

1. Fold a piece of dark-blue construction paper (9" x 12") in half lengthwise.
2. Fold a piece of light-blue ditto paper (8½" x 11") in half lengthwise.
3. On top half of light-blue paper, draw and color seaweed. Mount on dark-blue paper.
4. Cut four strips of construction paper 1" wide and a variety of lengths for each student. Fold into a rectangle or square and paste into the fold of light-blue paper.
5. Duplicate large fish patterns (four per student) on different colors of construction paper. Cut out.

6. Fill in pertinent information on small fish patterns and duplicate. Cut out.

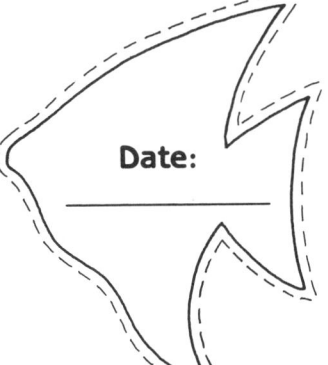
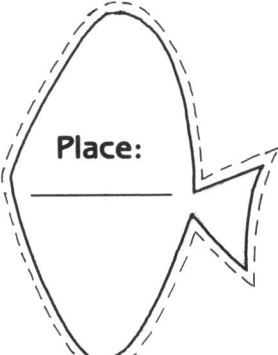
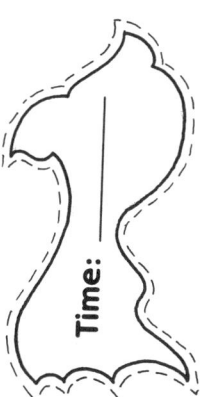

Date: ___   Place: ___   Time: ___   Please Bring: ___

7. Paste small fish onto large fish. Paste fish onto fronts of rectangles.

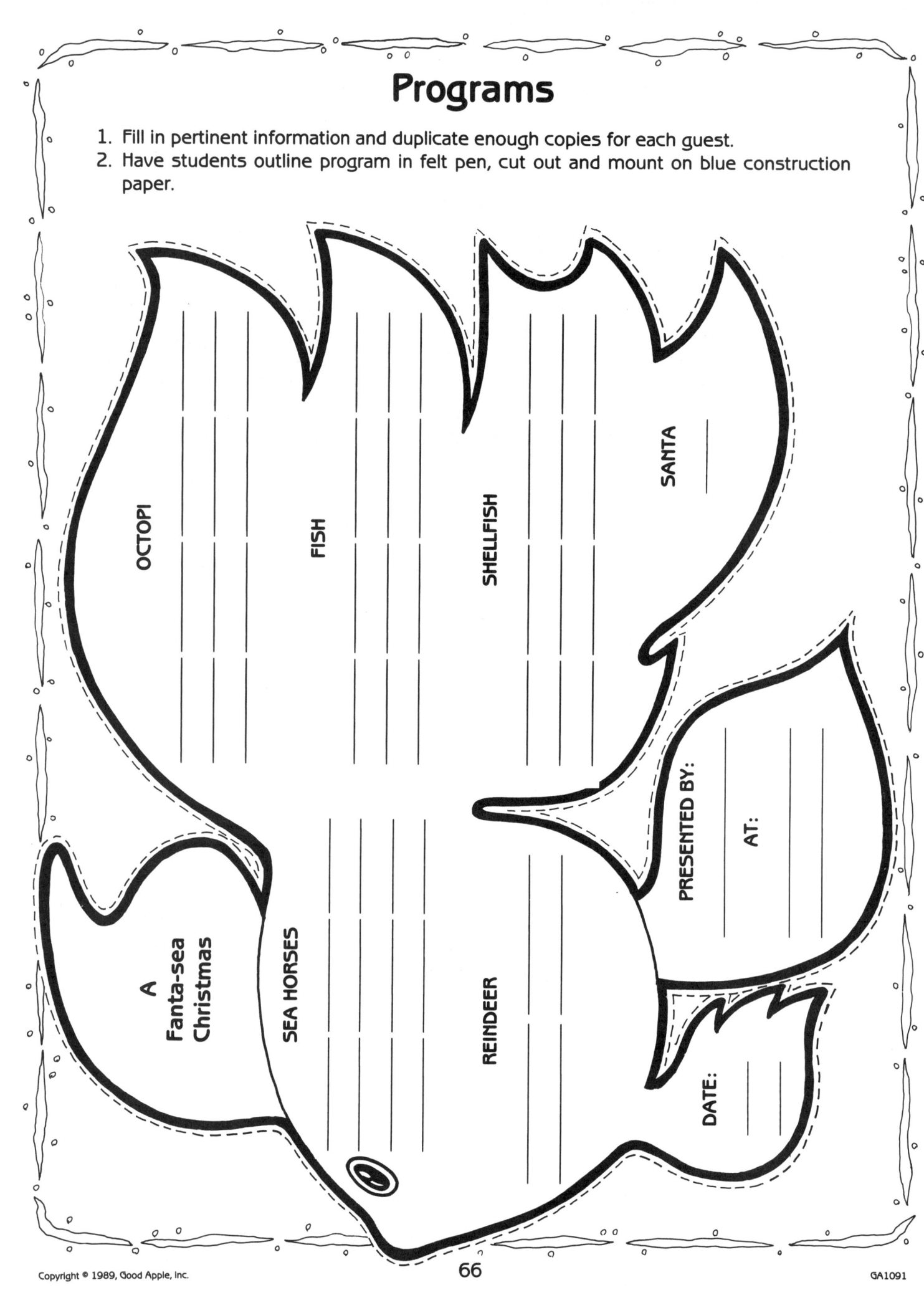

Decorations

Door Decoration

Make "A Fanta-sea Christmas" sign on large fish and hang on door.

Room Decorations

1. Have students work in pairs to create stuffed fish. Enlarge different fish patterns onto mural paper. Have students paint, outline in black and cut out. Turn over and trace shape onto another piece of mural paper. Paint, outline in black and cut out. Staple two sides almost all the way around and stuff with newspaper. Staple remainder of fish. Attach a piece of string to top and hang from the ceiling.

2. Hang strips of crepe paper from ceiling and windows to represent seaweed.

3. Create an undersea mural. On blue mural paper, have students draw and color with chalk tall pieces of seaweed. Fold *Reader's Digest* magazine pages. Fold right corner down to center then fold page in half. Spray with orange, red and/or green spray paint. Make eyes and tail fins with construction paper and staple to mural.

Name Tags

Parents or invited guests wear name tags corresponding to their child's part in the concert. Teacher duplicates a name tag for each guest.

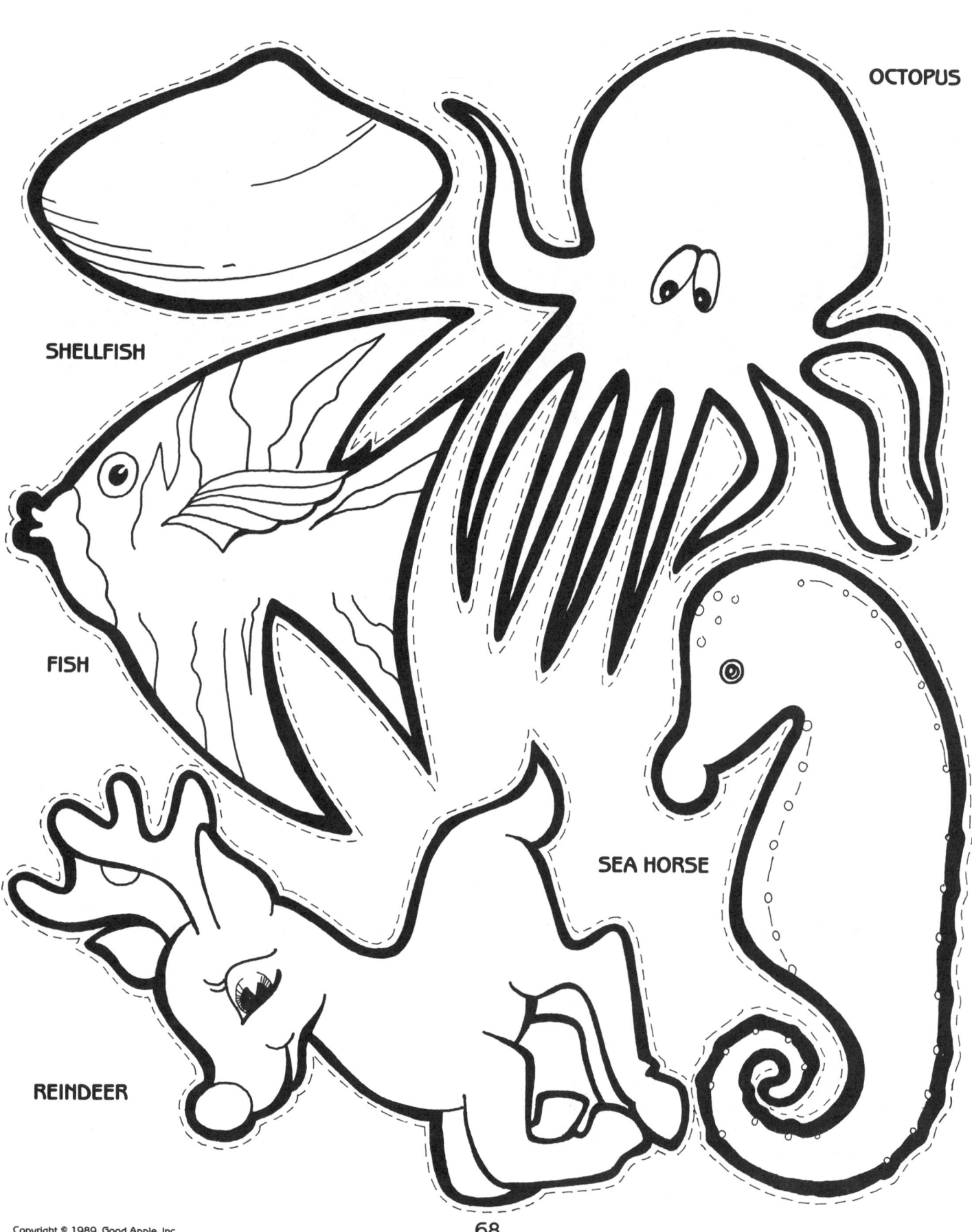

Refreshments

Parents are asked to bring (via the invitation) a refreshment item for after the concert. All refreshments are to be put on a central table for everyone to help themselves.

Fishy Foods

1. Clam chowder: Make together as a class project before the concert or have parents bring it.
2. Fish-shaped croutons for adding to clam chowder
3. Fish-shaped crackers topped with cream cheese and seafood
4. Seafood sandwiches (for example, tuna, salmon, shrimp, crab)
5. Raw vegetables presented on a fish platter
6. Shrimp-flavored chips and seafood cheese ball
7. A variety of dips (for example, shrimp dip, crab dip)
8. Make sugar cookies with class. Cut shapes with fish cookie cutter. Make a small hole at mouth of fish.
9. Lime punch (Optional: ice cubes with green cherries in the center)
10. Coffee, tea

Centerpiece

Cut a piece of Styrofoam into a boat shape. Cover with tinfoil. With needle and thread, attach fish cookie to straw of bamboo skewer to represent fish pole. Stick straws into Styrofoam boat. Stick one straw upright in the middle and attach sign "Fishy Foods."

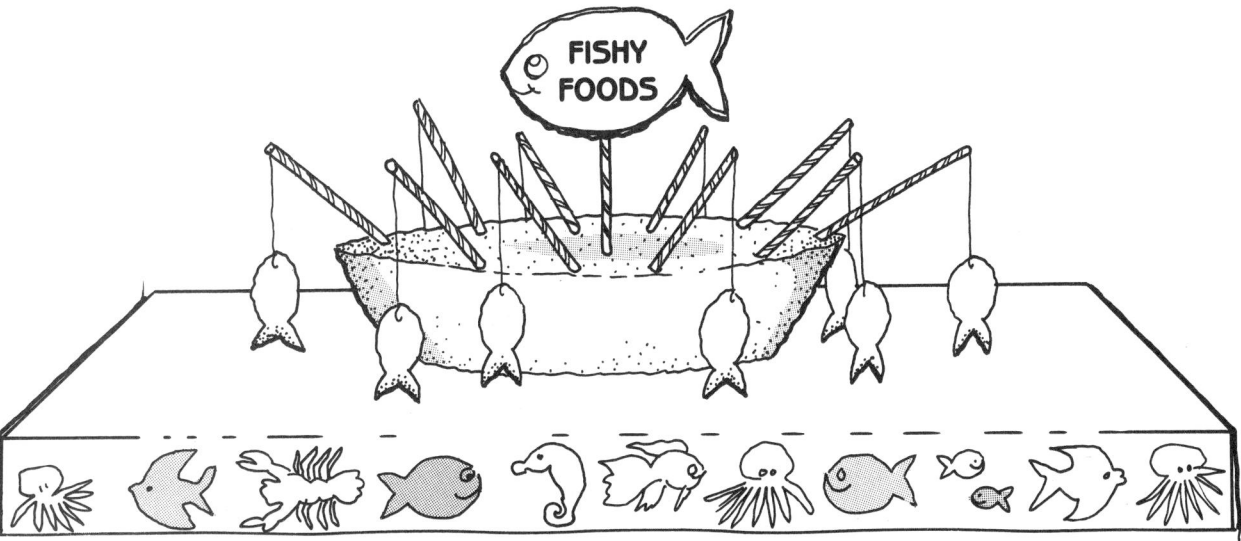

Refreshment Table

Cover table with blue mural paper. Have students draw and color a variety of small fish. Attach to bottom edge of tablecloth.

An International Christmas

(for a large primary grouping)

The concert starts at the North Pole with reindeer, elves and Santa getting ready for Santa's big trip delivering presents around the world on Christmas Eve. When he is finally ready, Santa then takes his audience to every continent of the world where they come upon many diverse and wonderful surprises which are unique to that specific continent. So travel the world with Santa on Christmas Eve and have an international Christmas!

The following is a guideline for assigning parts:

Characters	Songs	Music (to the tune of)	Suggested Grade
Reindeer	"The Reindeer"	"Captain Santa Claus"	2
Elves Santa	"Travelling the World"	"Santa Claus Is Coming to Town"	3
Foods	"Europe"	"Suzy Snowflake"	1
African Animals	"Africa"	"Rudolph the Red-Nosed Reindeer"	2
Panda Bears	"Asia"	"Frosty the Snowman"	1
Australian Animals	"Australia"	"Here Comes Santa Claus"	K
Penguins Icebergs	"Antarctica"	"Rockin' Around the Christmas Tree"	2
Coffee Machine Llamas Oil Rigs	"South America"	"Deck the Halls"	K
Professions	"North American Professions"	"Thirty-Two Feet and Eight Little Tails"	3
Cities	"North American Cities"	"Up on the Housetop"	All
Finale	"Travelling the World"	"Santa Claus Is Coming to Town"	All

Time Chart

This time chart will allow you to plan in advance all the activities involved in making "An International Christmas" a success.

October
Week 3: teacher familiarizes self with concert
Week 4: teacher gets song sheets and overhead transparencies ready for students to learn from

November
Week 1: start teaching concert songs
Week 2: start making decorations for gym
Week 3: start learning actions to songs
Week 4: start making costumes and props

December
Week 1: start practicing concert on stage, make invitations and send home
Week 2: make programs
Week 3: make sure everything is ready

Day Before Concert
Dress rehearsal

Day of Concert
Final dress rehearsal
Set up chairs in gym for audience
Decorate gym
Set up refreshment table and eating tables

Concert Time
Stay calm!

Notes to the Teacher

1. Each of the songs in the concert is suitable for any primary grade grouping.

2. The actions for each song are quite detailed. Depending on your teaching situation, you may choose to make some of the actions simpler.

3. For this primary concert, it is advisable to have several older students or adults acting as a stage crew as there are several props which need to be put on the stage and then taken off.

4. With the children being quite young, you have the choice of leading your students into their positions as well as standing on the floor and leading your class through their specific concert song and actions.

The Reindeer

(North Pole sign on stage to tell time of year and setting)
1. Reindeer enter running into positions on stage.
2. Students sing song twice, following actions on action sheet.
3. At the end of the song, students walk and take their places sitting on top two rows of choir risers at the back of the stage.
4. Eight students and Rudolph stay behind and take their places, sitting in formation in front of the sleigh.
5. One student from risers carries North Pole sign off stage.

Song #1

The Reindeer
(sung to the tune of "Captain Santa Claus")

Three cheers for Rudolph our hero,
He's at the top of our list
For making Christmas real special,
Something we don't want to miss.
His job is to lead our team,
With all his might and care,
And pull the sleigh and all those toys
Around everywhere.
We really wish we had a nose
That glowed red all day long,
But we know Santa likes us all
'Cuz we're brave and extra strong.
We love to fly up in the sky and all over the land.
With Rudolph at the helm,
We are in very good hands.

Actions

Three cheers for Rudolph our hero,
(raise right hand up over head)

He's at the top of our list
(point to Rudolph)

For making Christmas real special,
(pretend to hug self)

Something we don't want to miss.
(shake head back and forth in disagreement)

His job is to lead our team,
(point to Rudolph and then to self)

With all his might and care,
(raise right hand and then left to form a V)

And pull the sleigh and all those toys
(pretend to pull sleigh; jog in place)

Around everywhere.
(pretend to pull)

We really wish we had a nose
(stop jogging; point to nose with right index finger)

That glowed red all day long,
(make back and forth motion with index finger touching nose)

But we know Santa likes us all
(both arms out to side)

'Cuz we're brave and extra strong.
(pretend to flex muscles)

We love to fly up in the sky and all over the land.
(start jogging to the beat of the music)

With Rudolph at the helm,
(keep jogging and point to Rudolph)

We are in very good hands.
(stop jogging, stretch both hands out to side)

Actions for Rudolph

While other Reindeer are singing, Rudolph does his own actions—checks sleigh, flexes muscles, does knee bend, waves to audience.

Costumes and Props

Reindeer

Body: Wear brown shirts, brown pants and brown gloves. Trim with garland.

Antlers: Cut antlers out of heavyweight cardboard. Attach to headband or hanger bent to fit the head.

Optional Makeup: Use professional brown or powder paint, painted on facial foundation cream.

Rudolph: Same costume as above except with a red nose.

Nose: Paint nose red or use a clown's sponge nose or a flashing red bulb hooked up to batteries and secure on the student's head and face.

Sleigh

1. Use a gym storage box on wheels.
2. Cut out two heavy cardboard pieces in the shape of the side of a Christmas sleigh. Attach to each side of box. Paint in Christmas colors and trim with garland.
3. Attach two large ropes to front end of the sleigh to enable pulling of the sleigh by reindeer.

Map of the World
Place inside Santa's sleigh.

Posters

Posters are to be placed inside the sleigh to be picked up by Santa Claus and shown to the audience as he arrives on each new continent throughout the concert.

1. Well, hello there, Europe!
2. Merry Christmas, Africa!
3. Hi there, Asia!
4. Season's Greetings, Australia!
5. Salutations, Antarctica!
6. Best wishes, South America!
7. Howdy, North America!
8. Now it's back to the North Pole.

North Pole Sign
Attach sign onto a high jump standard.

Setting: North Pole
Time: Early Christmas Eve

Staging

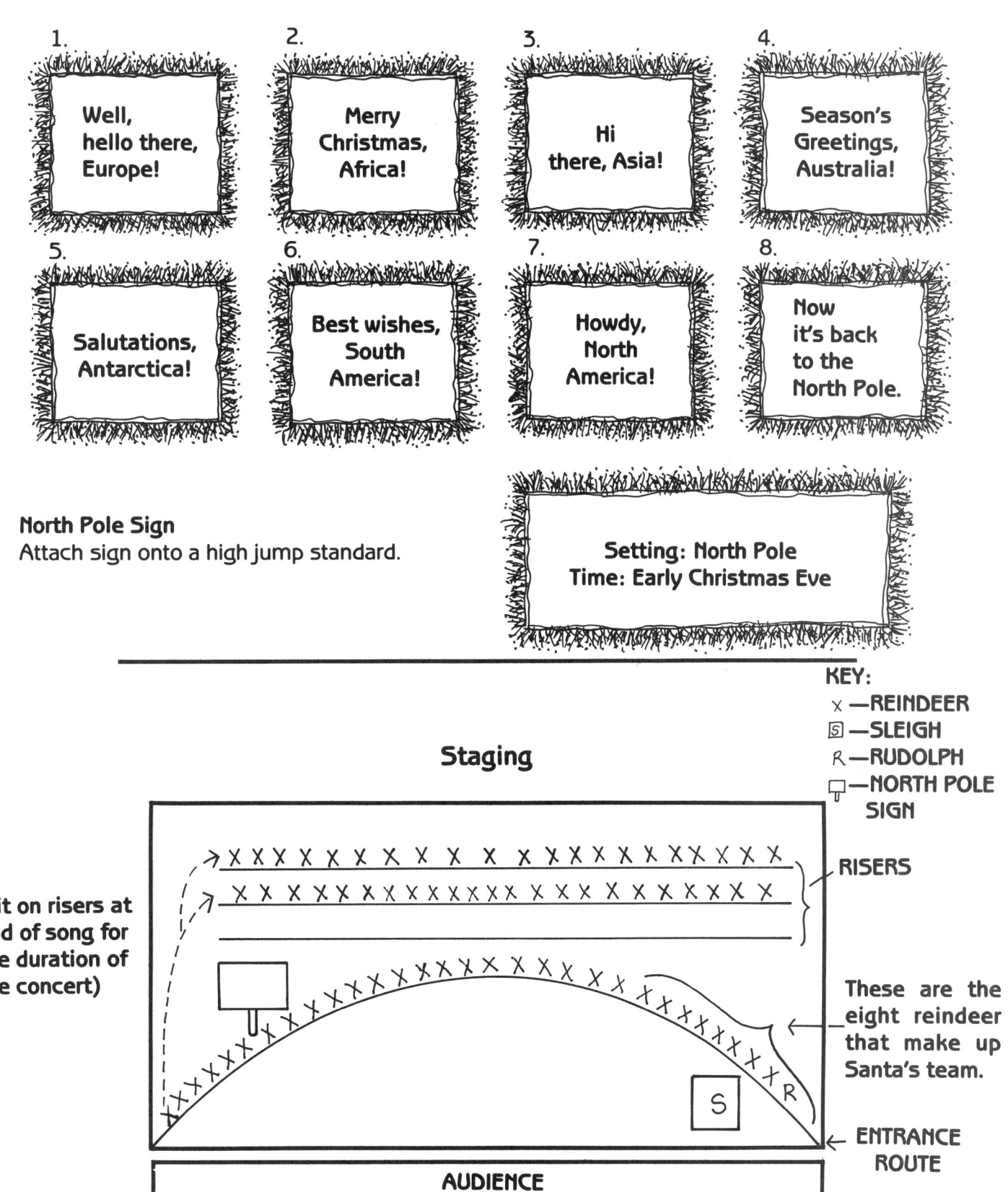

KEY:
- X — REINDEER
- S — SLEIGH
- R — RUDOLPH
- ⛳ — NORTH POLE SIGN

RISERS

(sit on risers at end of song for the duration of the concert)

These are the eight reindeer that make up Santa's team.

ENTRANCE ROUTE

AUDIENCE

Travelling the World

1. The Elves enter carrying presents (hidden from audience) and take staggered kneeling position on stage. They then put the presents in front of them on the floor and pretend to finish wrapping them. One student signals others. Students stand, walk and put presents in sleigh and take their standing positions for concert song.

2. Enter Santa Claus saying "Ho! Ho! Ho!" and waving to the audience. He walks around sleigh, pretending to check everything out. He then gets inside sleigh, sits down, takes out large map of the world and starts to read it.

3. Students sing song through two times and do accompanying actions while Santa is reading his map.

4. At the end of the song, students walk to their riser positions and remain there until the end of concert.

5. Santa's reindeer team pulls Santa across to the other side of stage. Santa continues to wave. The team turns the sleigh around, sits down and Santa gets out of the sleigh.

"Traveling the World" is sung after every song while Santa is being pulled across the stage.

Song #2
Travelling the World
(sung to the tune of "Santa Claus Is Coming to Town")

He's checked in his sleigh,
He's heading out,
Right on his way,
To points north and south,
Travelling the wor-rld is great.
He'll be heading east and then to points west,
Taking Christmas cheer to all the best,
Travelling the wor-rld is great.
It doesn't even matter,
Which land he first heads to,
For all the lands have really neat things,
To see by us and you.
He's checked in his sleigh,
He's heading out,
Right on his way,

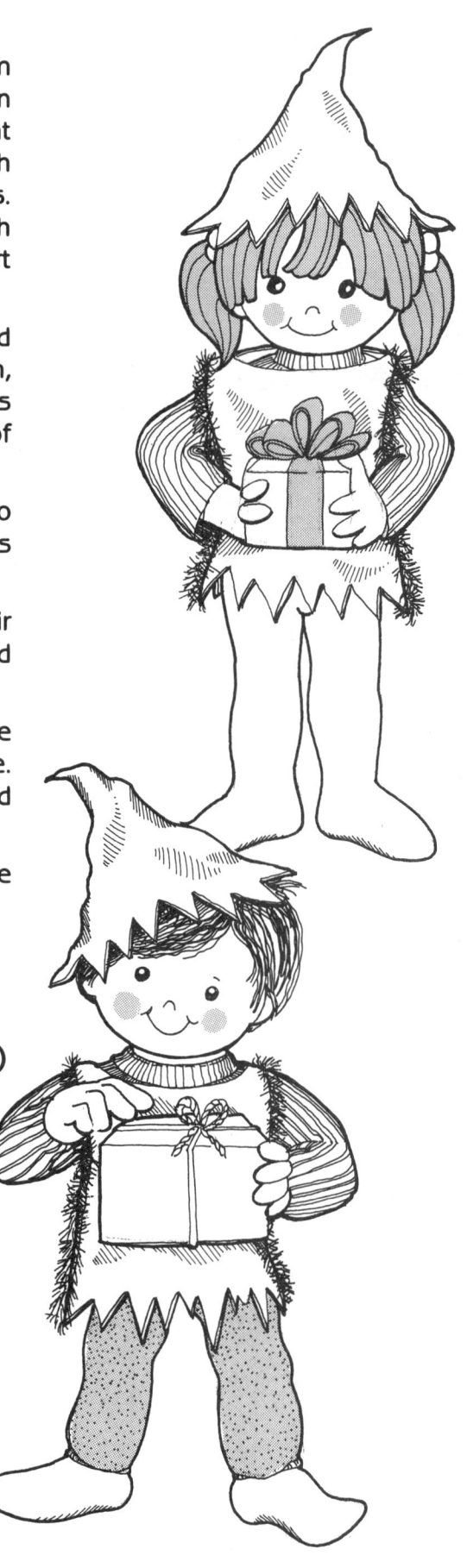

Actions

He's checked in his sleigh,
(right hand over right eyebrow, pretend to check around oneself)

He's heading out,
(point right hand out into the audience)

Right on his way,
(roll two hands, one over the other in front of self)

To points north and south,
(right arm points up and then down)

Travelling the wor-rld is great.
(make large circular motion with right arm going clockwise)

He'll be heading east and then to points west,
(right arm points right and then left)

Taking Christmas cheer to all the best,
(right hand traces out large smile on own face)

Travelling the wor-rld is great.
(large circular arm motion)

It doesn't even matter,
(shake head to the side)

Which land he first heads to,
(right arm out, together with other students, point in different directions)

For all the lands have really neat things,
(pretend to hug oneself)

To see by us and you.
(both arms point to audience then both arms point to self)

He's checked in his sleigh,
(right hand over right eyebrow)

He's heading out,
(point right hand into audience again)

Right on his way,
(roll hands again)

To points north and south,
(right arm points again)

Travelling the wor-rld is great.
(large circular motion again)

Costumes and Props

Elves
In matching dark colors, girls wear gym tights and boys wear sweatpants. Wear turtleneck sweaters. Make vests out of green mural paper and hang around neck. Make green construction paper pixie hats. Trim with garland. Wear rouge on cheeks if you wish.

Santa Claus
Use a professional suit if available. If not, trim a red jogging suit, red flannel hat and construction paper beard with cotton batting. Wear a black belt, black boots, white wig, and white gloves. Wear rouge on cheeks.

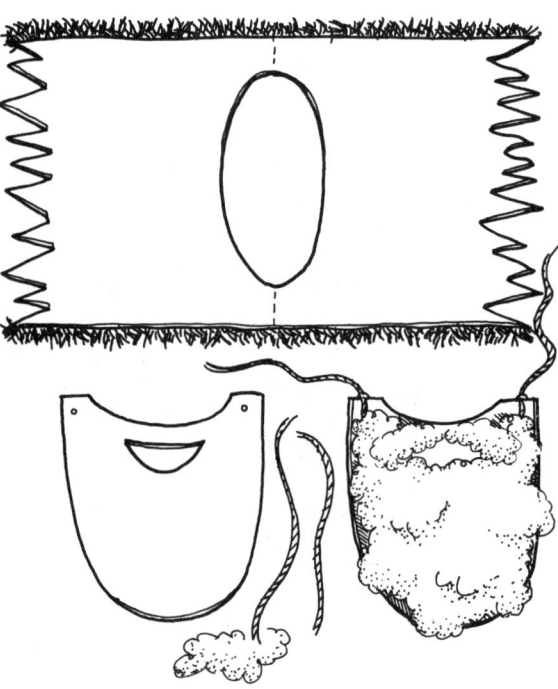

Staging

OPENING KNEELING POSITIONS

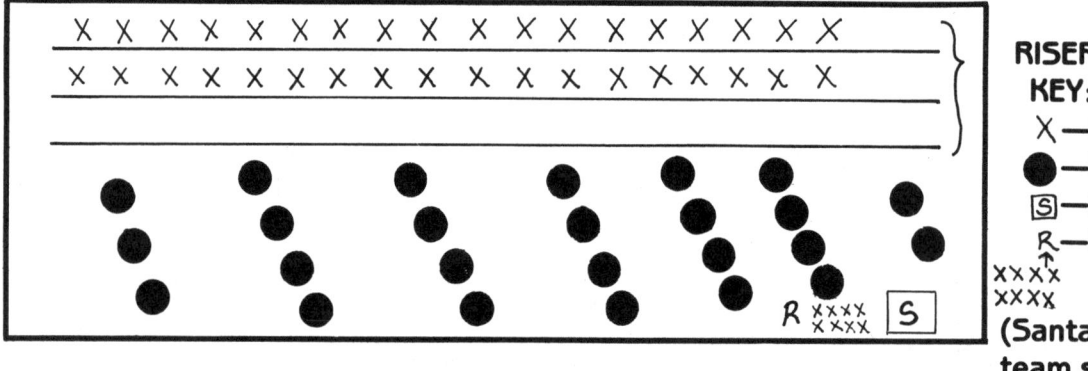

RISERS KEY:
- X — REINDEER
- ● — ELVES
- S — SLEIGH
- R — RUDOLPH

(Santa's reindeer team sit until end of song)

STANDING POSITIONS FOR CONCERT

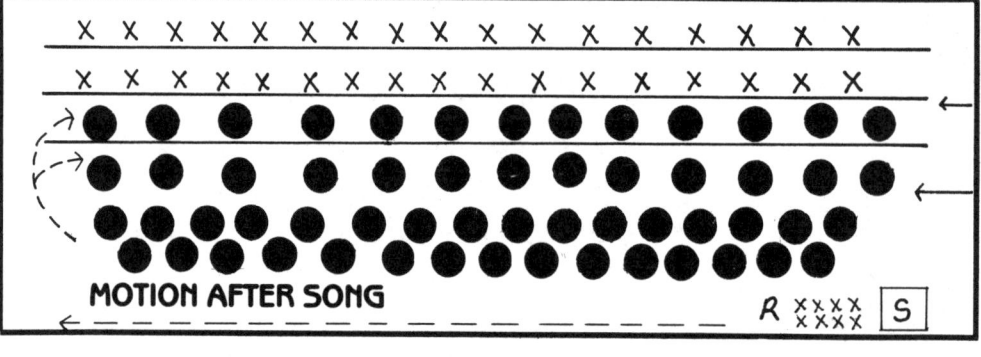

← sitting down for duration of concert

← sitting cross-legged on floor for duration of concert

Europe

1. Santa continues to wave to the audience. He reaches into his sleigh and pulls out poster #1. "Well hello there, Europe." He shows it to the audience, pretends to get a few presents out of the sleigh, takes place back in sleigh and continues to read the map.

2. Enter students. Take positions on stage and sing song through twice while doing accompanying actions.

3. At end of song, students exit off the stage to left.

4. Elves and Reindeer on risers immediately start to sing song #2, "Travelling the World," once through. They do the actions for the song while they're sitting down.

5. Santa puts map away. His team pulls him across stage while song #2 is being sung. The team turns the sleigh around when they reach the other side of the gym. Santa gets out of his sleigh.

Song #3

Europe
(sung to the tune of "Suzy Snowflake")

Eu-rope is a great place,
W-welcome to you all.
Paris, Rome and London and the rest
Have lots of real good tastes.
Eu-rope has such great food,
We know that you'll agree,
Pizza, spaghetti and fish and chips
Are as good as they can be.
If you want to taste some herring,
Sweden's the place that you should see.
If you want to taste some schnitzel,
Go—to Germany.
Eu-rope is a great place,
There's every type of food,
French bread, pastries and borscht as well,
To put you in the mood.

Actions

Eu-rope is a great place,
(one step forward)

W-welcome to you all.
(wave to audience)

Paris, Rome and London and the rest
(one step back)

Have lots of real good tastes.
(pretend to rub stomach)

Eu-rope has such great food,
(pretend to eat)

We know that you'll agree,
(both hands outstretched to audience)

Pizza, spaghetti and fish and chips
(students who are these three foods take one step forward)

Are as good as they can be.
(all students nod heads up and down)

If you want to taste some herring,
(herring takes one step forward)

Sweden's the place that you should see,
(right hand over eyebrows, pretend to look)

If you want to taste some schnitzel,
(schnitzel takes one step forward)

Go—to Germany.
(right hand pointing out to audience)

Eu-rope is a great place,
(all remaining students take one step forward)

There's every type of food,
(move costume to right and then to left)

French bread, pastries and borscht as well,
(continue to move costume in time to the music)

To put you in the mood.
(continue moving costume)

Staging

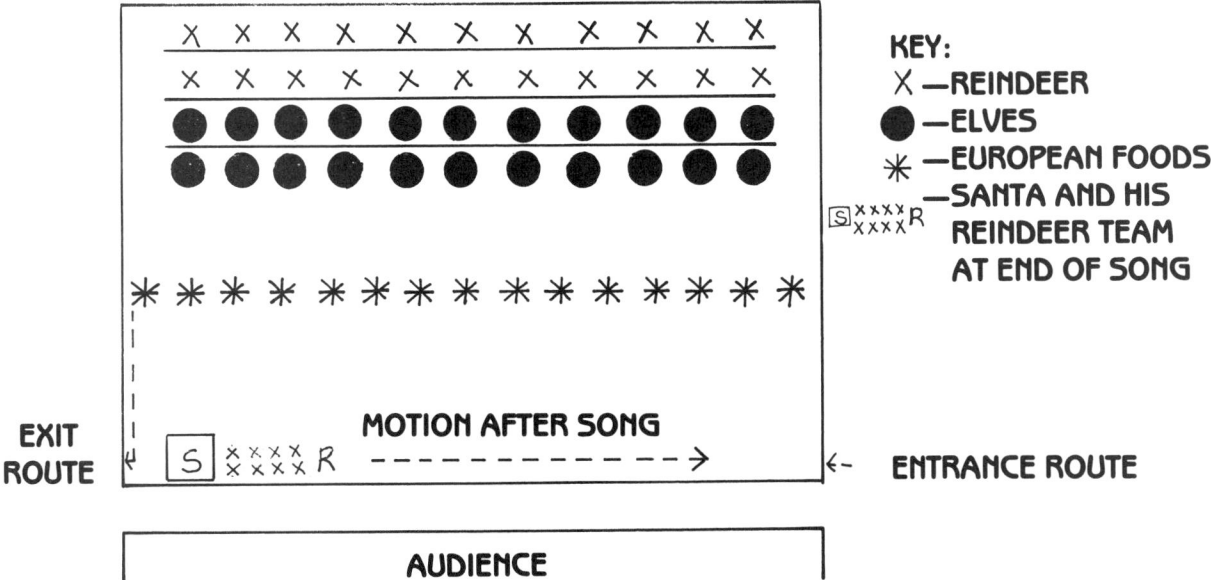

Costumes and Props

European Foods
Each student wears a large piece of heavyweight cardboard around neck. Make an overhead transparency of each of the following patterns; then trace the sketches onto the heavyweight cardboard. Students paint their own costumes and trim with garland.

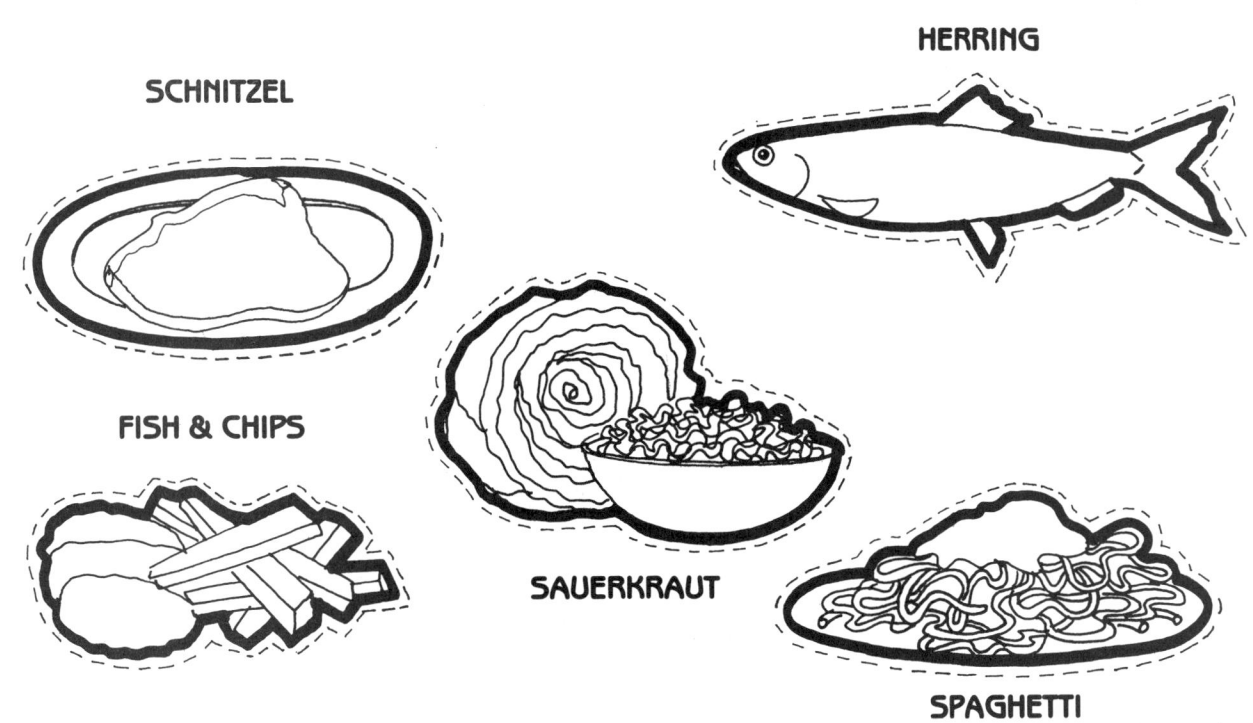

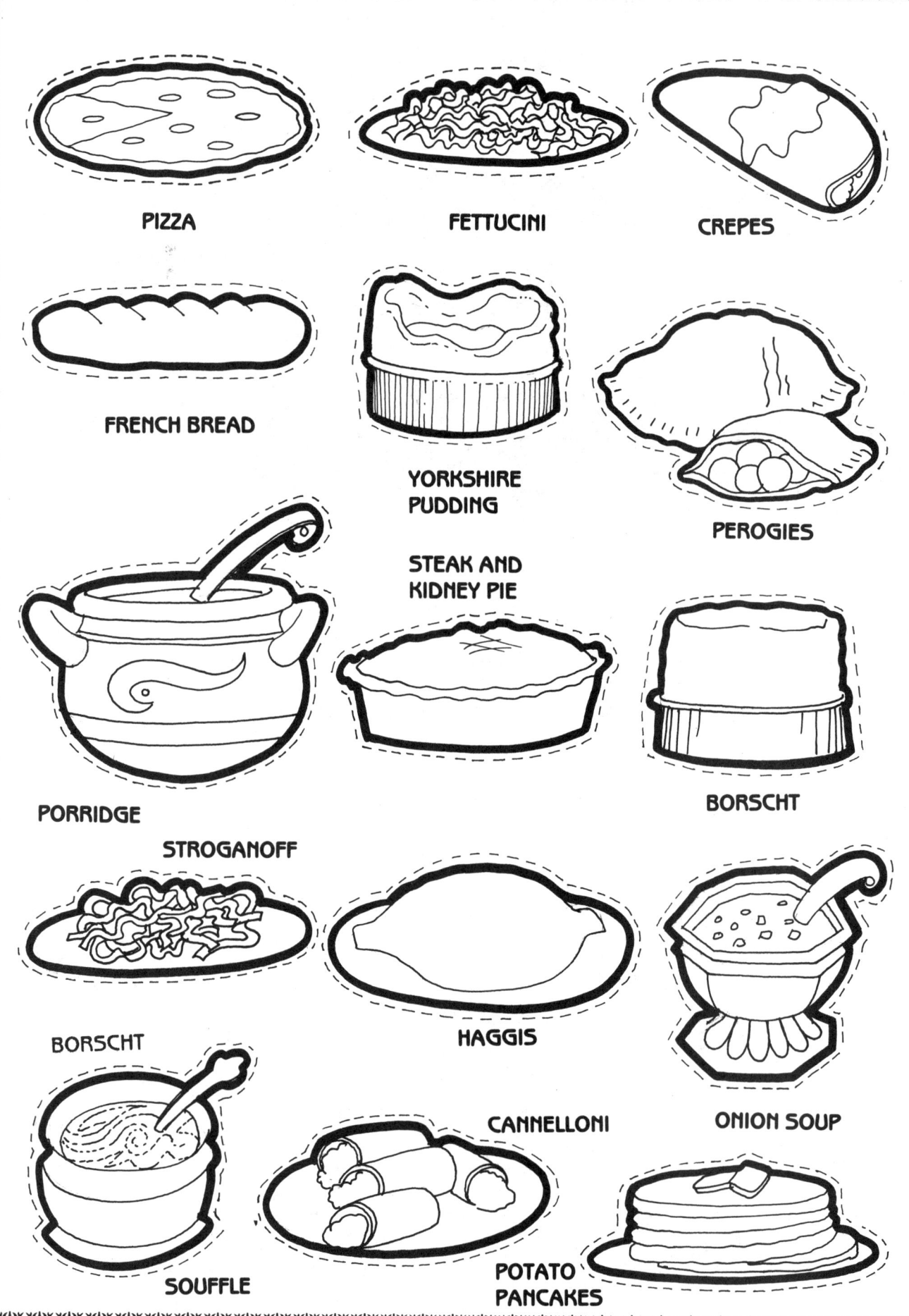

Africa

1. Santa continues to wave to the audience. He reaches into his sleigh and pulls out poster #2, "Merry Christmas, Africa!" He shows the audience the poster, pretends to get a few presents out of the sleigh, takes his place back in the sleigh and continues to read the map.

2. Enter students. Walk to front line formation and sing song through twice while doing accompanying actions.

3. At the end of the song, students exit stage left.

4. Elves and Reindeer sing song #2 sitting down once while doing accompanying actions.

5. Santa's team pulls Santa across stage while song #2 is being sung. The sleigh is then turned around. Santa gets out of sleigh.

Song #4

Africa

(sung to the tune of "Rudolph the Red-Nosed Reindeer")

We are lions and tigers and monkeys and rhinos,
Giraffes and zebras and 'gators and hippos;
Some of us are small, while the rest are la-arge and tall.
Africa is our country;
All of us like living there
On the plains or in the jungles,
With our share of clean fresh air.
Africa is our homeland;
Come along and you will see,
All the fun that you can have
On a great big Sa-far-i.
Giraffes roam around the plains
With their necks up high,
Hippos wallow in the mud,
'Gators like it when it floods.
All the cats stalk the grasslands,
Monkeys play up in the trees,
Africa is our country—
It's a place where we can live free.

Actions

We are lions and tigers and monkeys and rhinos,
Giraffes and zebras and 'gators and hippos;
(each animal wiggles its costume back and forth when its name is mentioned)

Some of us are small, while the rest are la-arge and tall.
(small animals wiggle costumes; then large animals wiggle costumes)

Africa is our country; all of us like living there
(one step forward)   (one step back)

On the plains or in the jungles,
(move one step to the right)

With our share of clean fresh air.
(move one step to the left)

Africa is our homeland;
(move one step forward)

Come along and you will see,
(move one step back)

All the fun that you can have
(move one step to the right)

On a great big Sa-far-i.
(move one step to the left)

Giraffes roam around the plains with their necks up high,
(Giraffes move one step forward)

Hippos wallow in the mud,
(Hippos move one step forward)

'Gators like it when it floods.
(Alligators move one step forward)

All the cats stalk the grasslands,
(all Wild Cats move one step forward)

Monkeys play up in the trees,
(Monkeys move one step forward)

Africa is our country—
(all other animals move one step forward)

It's a place where we can live free.
(stand still and wiggle costumes back and forth)

Staging

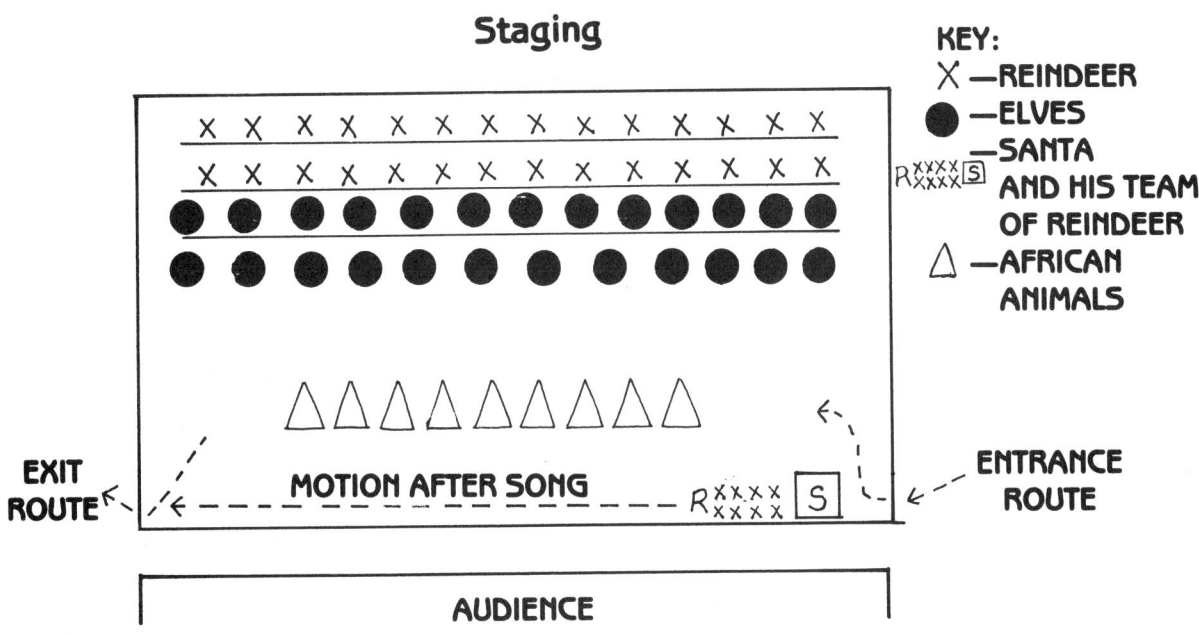

Costumes and Props

1. Make a transparency of the following patterns and enlarge onto large pieces of corrugated cardboard so the size of each sketch reaches from the student's head down to his knees. Paint.
2. Put eye holes and mouth holes into cardboard.
3. Secure pieces of sewing elastic to back of head and stomach areas on cardboard.
4. Each student may then easily have animal figure held securely on his body. Student's hands may hold sides of cardboard animal.

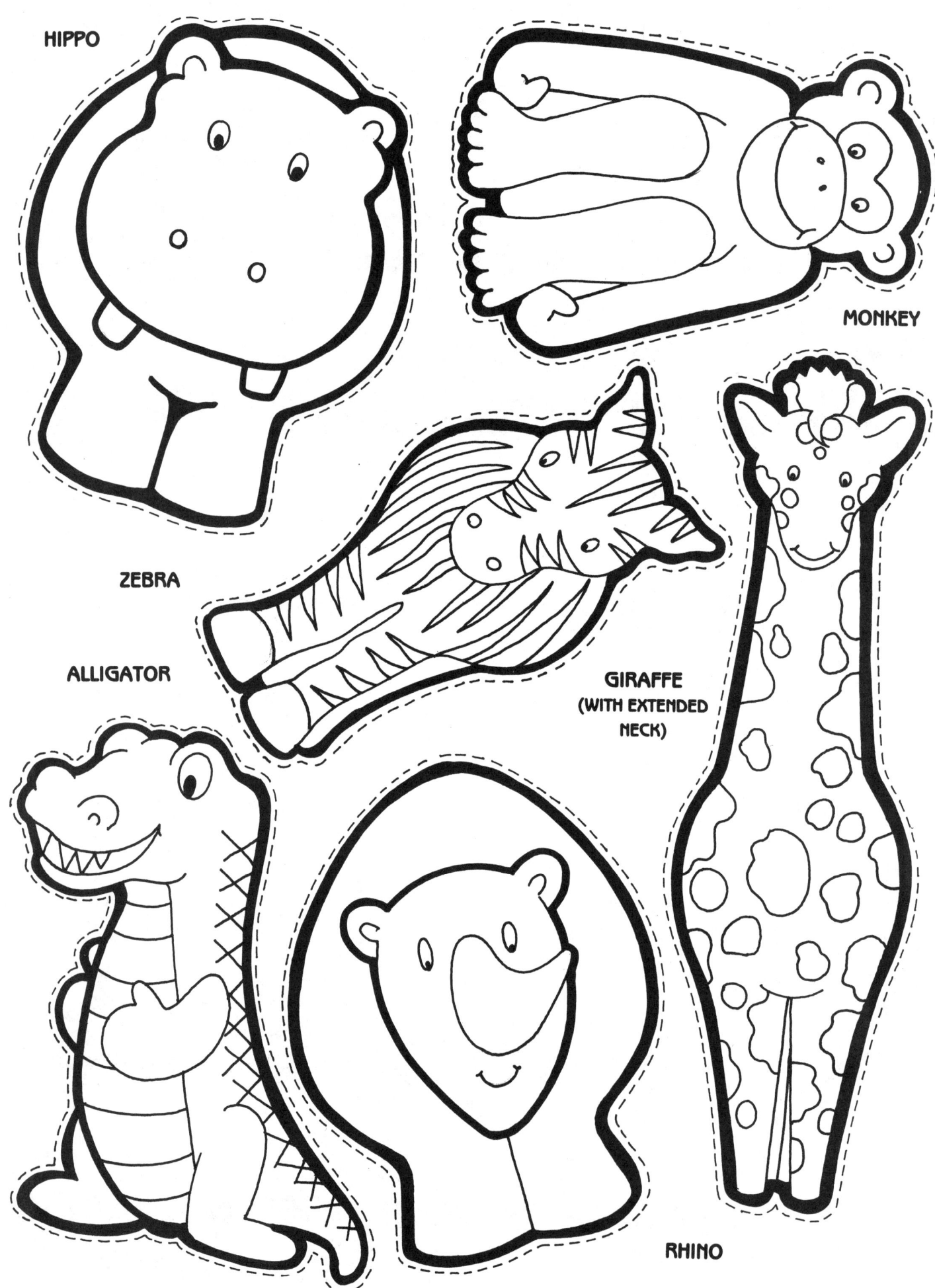

Asia

1. Santa reaches into sleigh and pulls out poster #3, "Hi there, Asia!" He shows the poster to the audience, pretends to get a few presents out of the sleigh, takes his place back in the sleigh and continues to read the map.
2. Enter half of the students carrying signs of Asian countries. They sit down with their legs hanging over the edge of the stage. They then sing first four lines of song.
3. On the fifth line Panda Bears enter and take their place on stage while singing remainder of song. The song is to be sung twice.
4. At the end of song, Sign Holders and Panda Bears exit stage left.
5. Elves and Reindeer sing song #2 once while doing actions.
6. Santa's team pulls Santa across the stage while song #2 is being sung. The sleigh is then turned around. Santa gets out of the sleigh.

Song #5

Asia

(sung to the tune of "Frosty the Snowman")

Countries of Asia are as neat as they can be,
The-ey all have things that we like a lot,
We know that you all agree.
Countries of Asia ha-ave something we like best,
It's the panda bear for which we sure care
Better than the rest.
It's black and white and so cute looking
That we can't resist,
Just wondering if we could put it on our Christmas list.
For pandas are gr-reat,
Whether they are stuffed or real,
And no matter when yo-ou look at them
Happy is how you will feel.

Chorus:
Panda Bear, Panda, Panda Bear, Panda,
Better than the rest.
Panda Bear, Panda, Panda Bear, Panda,
Better than the rest.

Actions

Countries of Asia are as neat as they can be,
(Sign Holders walk in singing and take their places)

The-ey all have things that we like a lot,
(They wave their signs as they sing until the end of line 4)

We know that you all agree.
Countries of Asia ha-ave something we like best,
(During the second singing, Panda Bears sit down and pretend to play until the end of line 4 when they stand up)

It's the panda bear for which we sure care
(enter Panda Bears lumbering along to form circle)

Better than the rest.
(lumber around in circle)

It's black and white and so cute looking
(lumber into straight line position)

That we can't resist,
(Pandas sit in bearlike fashion with legs reaching out)

Just wondering if we could put it on our Christmas list.
(Pandas stretch arms in a bearlike fashion)

For pandas are gr-reat,
(Pandas scratch tummies in bearlike fashion)

Whether they are stuffed or real,
(Pandas stand up)

And no matter when yo-ou look at them
(Pandas lumber around in small circle)

Happy is how you will feel.
(Pandas stand still and put paws up to show audience)

Chorus:
Panda Bear, Panda, Panda Bear, Panda,
Better than the rest.
(Sign Holders put their signs down and along with Pandas clap to the beat of the music)

Panda Bear, Panda, Panda Bear, Panda,
(keep clapping)

Better than the rest.
(keep clapping)

Costumes and Props

Sign Holders
Wear ordinary school clothes trimmed in garland.

Signs
Put the name of one Asian country on each sign. Paint in letters and trim with garland. Use countries such as Afghanistan, Japan, Philippines, China, Mongolia, Indochina, Taiwan, Burma, India, Thailand, Sri Lanka, Korea, Indonesia, Malaysia, etc.

Panda Bears
Wear black sweatpants and black sweatshirts. Make black ears and attach to coat hanger bent to fit shape of head. Wear white mittens to represent paws.

Optional Makeup: Apply thick facial cream all over face; then apply white tempera powder. Paint black tempera powder around eyes, around mouth and on nose.

Staging

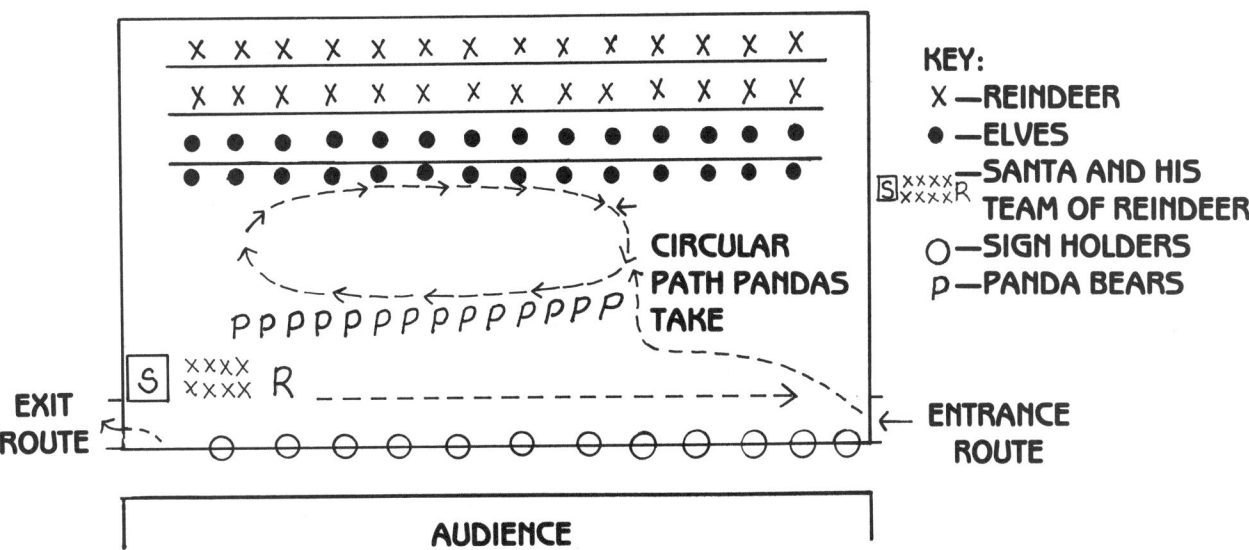

Australia

1. Santa reaches into his sleigh and pulls out poster #4, "Season's Greetings, Australia!" He shows the poster to the audience, pretends to get a few presents out of his sleigh, takes his place back in the sleigh and continues to read the map.
2. Enter students. They stand in a straight line formation and sing song twice while doing accompanying actions.
3. At the end of song, students exit stage left.
4. Elves and Reindeer sing song #2 once again while Santa is being pulled across stage.
5. The sleigh is turned around and Santa gets out of the sleigh.

Song #6

Australia
(sung to the tune of "Here Comes Santa Claus")

Verse 1:
We are koalas, we are kiwis,
We are kookaburras too,
From way down under in Austral-ia,
The Land of the Kangaroo.
We like cuddling, we like chirping,
We like hopping a-lot.
Australia's a-a-a real great place,
'Cuz there's lots to rave about.

Verse 2:
We are some turtles, we are some she-eep,
We are platypus-es,
From way down under in Austral-ia,
The place where everyone says,
We like swimming, we like baa-ing
And we like flat feet too,
Australia's a-a-a real great place,
So Mer-ry Christmas to you.

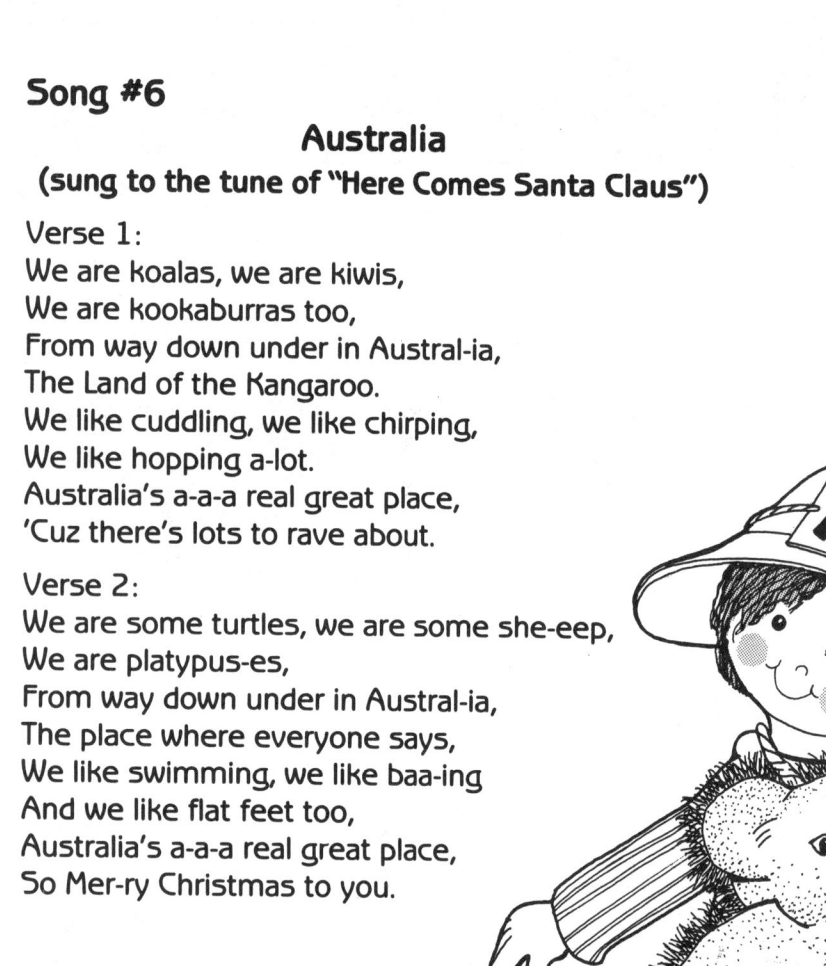

Actions

Verse 1:
We are koalas, we are kiwis,
(Koalas point to themselves, Kiwis point to themselves)

We are kookaburras too,
(Kookaburras point to themselves)

From way down under in Austral-ia,
(both hands point down)

The Land of the Kangaroo.
(Kangaroos point to themselves)

We like cuddling, we like chirping,
(pretend to cuddle, then hold right hand out; move right fingers to right thumb so as to show chirping motion)

We like hopping a-lot.
(hop once)

Australia's a-a-a real great place,
(both hands out to audience)

'Cuz there's lots to rave about.
(point to self)

Verse 2:
We are some turtles, we are some she-eep,
(Turtles point to themselves, Sheep point to themselves)

We are platypus-es,
(Platypuses point to themselves)

From way down under in Austral-ia,
(both hands point down)

The place where everyone says,
(cup right ear with right hand)

We like swimming, we like baa-ing
(pretend to breaststroke, Sheep baa)

And we like flat feet too,
(take two heavy steps)

Australia's a-a-a real great place,
(both hands out to audience)

So Mer-ry Christmas to you.
(point to hats)

Staging

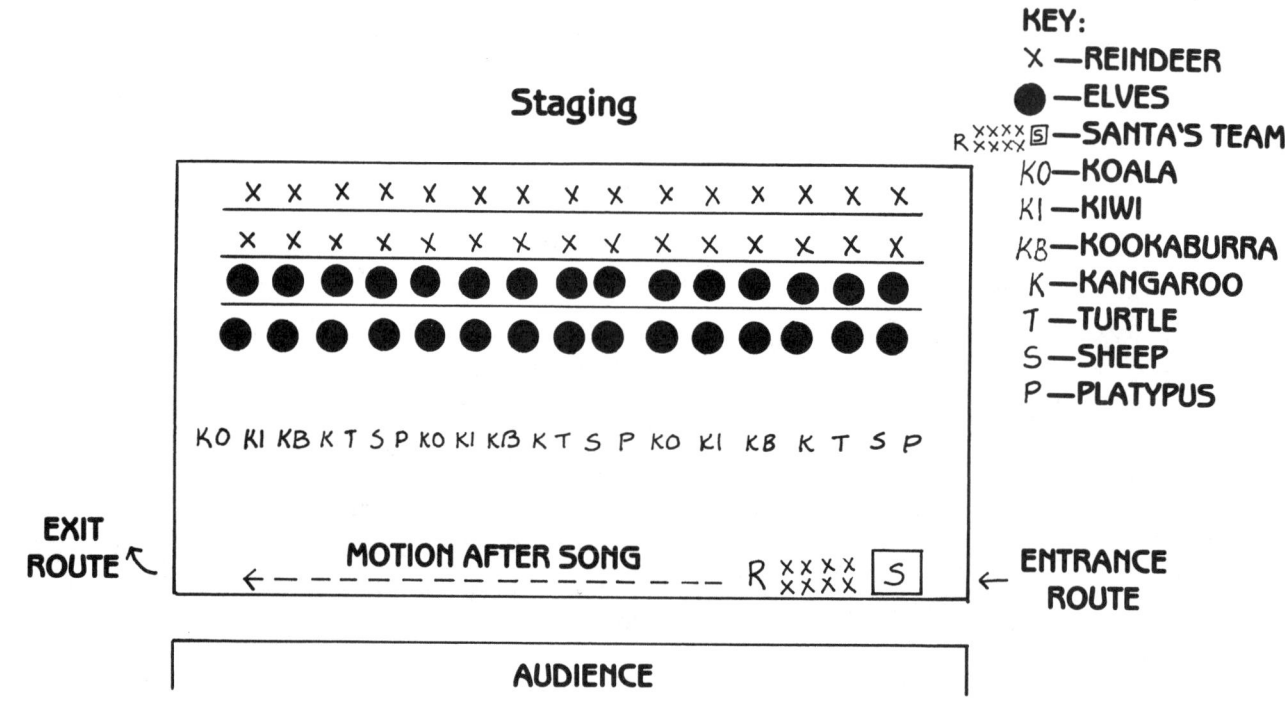

KEY:
- X — REINDEER
- ● — ELVES
- R XXXX S — SANTA'S TEAM
- KO — KOALA
- KI — KIWI
- KB — KOOKABURRA
- K — KANGAROO
- T — TURTLE
- S — SHEEP
- P — PLATYPUS

Costumes and Props

Australian Animals
Make an overhead transparency and make three enlargements of each pattern so each will fit the size of a large piece of railroad board. Have older student or parent helper paint costumes and trim with garland. Hang around neck with string.

Hats
Each student is to bring one hat from home (sun hat, baseball hat, etc.). Using pieces of cardboard with one letter painted on each, secure cardboard pieces onto the hat so that when students face the audience, the following Christmas message will be visible.

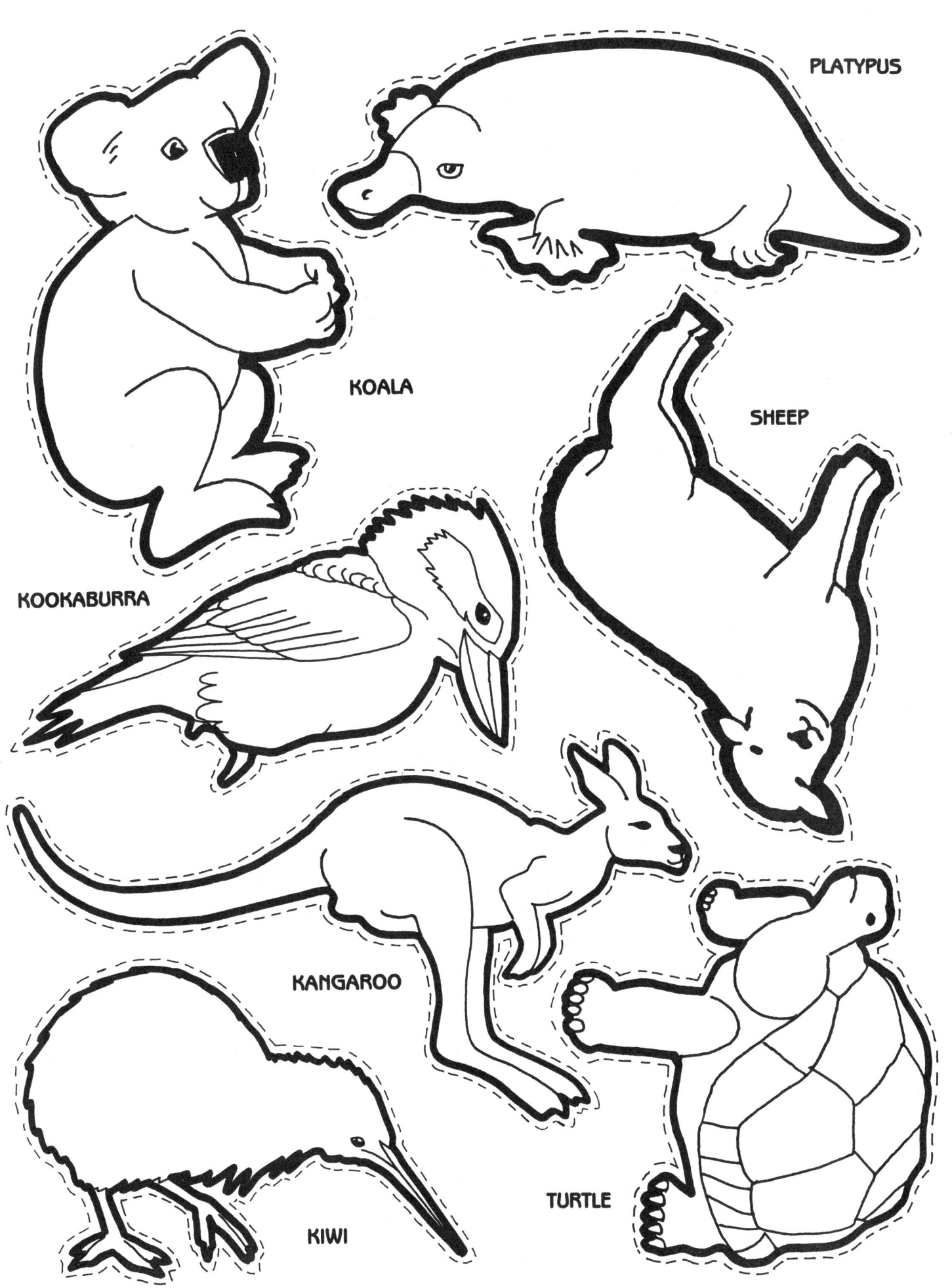

Antarctica

1. Santa reaches into his sleigh and pulls out poster #5, "Salutations, Antarctica!" He shows the poster to the audience, pretends to get a few presents out of his sleigh and continues to read the map.
2. Enter students. They take their stage positions and sing their song through twice while doing actions.
3. At the end of the song, students exit stage left.
4. Elves and Reindeer sing song #2 once again while Santa is being pulled across stage.
5. The sleigh is turned around. Santa gets out of the sleigh.

Song #7

Antarctica
(sung to the tune of "Rockin' Around the Christmas Tree")

W-welcome to the cold South Pole,
Where we have such fun on ice,
Sliding and flapping all a-round;
We sure think it's extra nice.
W-welcome to the cold South Pole,
Where we rarely see the sun,
But we don't care 'cuz we prefer
Cold conditions for our fun.
We love the cold nights
And the big supply of fresh fish.
Frozen fishes happen to be—WOW!
Our tastiest and best dish.
W-welcome to the frozen South,
We-ee wish you could see us,
Every day we can surely say,
It's tru-ly Chirst-mas.

Actions

P = Penguins (make small brisk waddling steps for the entire song)

I = Icebergs

W-welcome to the cold South Pole,
(P: stretch arms out to audience, I: wiggle costume back and forth)

Where we have such fun on ice,
(P: turn around once to left, I: wiggle costume)

Sliding and flapping all a-round;
(P: flap straight arms against sides, I: step to left then to right)

We sure think it's extra nice.
(P: flap so hands touch, I: step to left then to right)

W-welcome to the cold South Pole,
(P: arms outstretched to audience, I: wiggle costume)

Where we rarely see the sun,
(P: right arm points up, shake head "no," I: wiggle costume)

But we don't care 'cuz we prefer
(P: roll hands over each other, I: take one step forward)

Cold conditions for our fun.
(P: wrap arms around self and shiver, I: take one step back)

We love the cold nights
(P: move in circular path around stage for next three lines, I: wiggle costume)

And the big supply of fresh fish.
(P: keep moving, I: keep wiggling)

Frozen fishes happen to be—WOW!
(P: keep moving, I: jog in place)

Our tastiest and best dish.
(P: rub tummy in circular motion, I: wiggle costume)

W-welcome to the frozen South,
We-ee wish you could see us,
(P: turn once to left, I: wiggle costume)

Every day we can surely say,
(P: turn once to right, I: step to left)

It's tru-ly Christ-mas.
(P: flap hands together, I: step to the right)

Costumes and Props

Penguins

Body:	Wear black turtlenecks, black pants, white gloves and dark running shoes.
Nose:	Make a beak from yellow construction paper folded in half and cut into the shape of a beak. Beak can be secured to head with elastic.
Chest:	Cut white mural paper into the shape of a penguin's chest and attach to body by tying a string around the neck.
Optional Makeup:	Apply thick facial cream to face. Put black tempera paint on top of facial cream. Paint white tempera around eyes.

Icebergs

Cut out large jagged, heavy cardboard forms painted white to represent large sections of ice. Student holds iceberg pieces with both arms. These pieces of ice should reach from the student's shoulders down to his knees.

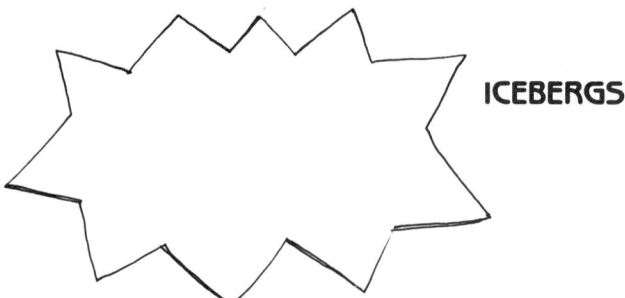

Staging

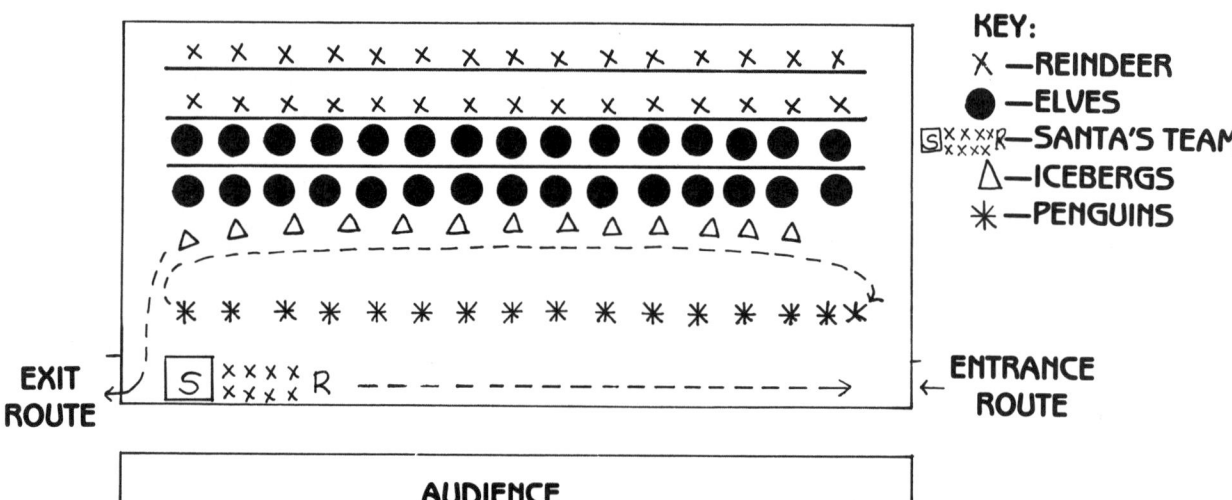

South America

1. Stage crew puts three large boxes on stage.
2. Santa reaches into sleigh and shows poster #6, "Best wishes, South America!" to the audience. He pretends to get a few presents out of the sleigh, gets back into sleigh and continues to read the map.
3. Enter students taking their positions on stage.
4. When the introduction of the song is played, students A and B turn box #1 around to show audience the painting of the large coffee machine.
5. All students sing verse 1 and do actions.
6. Just before verse 2, students C and D turn around box #2 to show the painting of a large llama.
7. All students sing verse 2 and do actions.
8. Just before verse 3, students E and F turn around box #3 to show the painting of a large oil rig.
9. All students sing the final verse and do actions.
10. At the end of the song, students exit stage left.
11. Elves and Reindeer sing song #2 while Santa is being pulled across stage.
12. The sleigh is turned around and Santa gets out of the sleigh.

Song #8

South America
(sung to the tune of "Deck the Halls")

South America has coffee,
Perk-a-perk-a-perk-drip-perk-perk-drip,
The best you can find in be-eans,
Perk-a-perk-a-perk-drip-perk-perk-drip,
Grind us up and you will see,
Perk-a-perk-a-perk-drip-perk-perk-drip,
All the best that coffee can be,
Perk-a-perk-a-perk-drip-perk-perk-drip.

South America has llamas,
Wooly-wooly-wool with necks so high,
Our coats make good pajamas,
Wooly-wooly-wool with necks so high,
We're as different as can be-ee,
Wooly-wool, wooly wool with necks so high,
Looking very graceful-ly,
Wooly-wooly-wool with necks so high.

South America has lots of oil,
Gush-a-gush-a-gush-gush-gush-gush-splurt,
Spurting fro-om under the soil,
Gush-a-gush-a-gush-gush-gush-gush-splurt,
We pump it out and barrel it,
Gush-a-gush-a-gush-gush-gush-gush-splurt,
With our crude we're really a hit,
Gush-a-gush-a-gush-gush-gush-gush-splurt.

Actions

South America has coffee,
(clap to the left and then right in time with the music)

Perk-a-perk-a-perk-drip-perk-perk-drip,
(bob head up and down in time with the music)

The best you can find in be-eans,
(repeat line 1)

Perk-a-perk-a-perk-drip-perk-perk-drip,
(bob head again)

Grind us up and you will see,
(pretend to crunch two hands together)

Perk-a-perk-a-perk-drip-perk-perk-drip,
(bob head again)

All the best that coffee can be,
(clapping action to the left and to the right)

Perk-a-perk-a-perk-drip-perk-perk-drip.
(bobbing action)

South America has llamas,
(clapping action)

Wooly-wooly-wool with necks so high,
(roll hands over each other then point both arms up)

Our coats make good pajamas,
(point to self)

Wooly-wooly-wool with necks so high,
(roll hands, point both arms up)

We're as different as can be-ee,
(clapping action)

Wooly-wool, wooly-wool with necks so high,
(roll hands, point both arms up)

Looking very graceful-ly,
(clapping action)

Wooly-wooly-wool with necks so high.
(roll hands, point both arms up)

South America has lots of oil,
(clapping action)

Gush-a-gush-a-gush-gush-gush-gush-splurt,
(alternate reaching left and right arm above head in time with the music)

Spurting fro-om under the soil,
(clapping action)

Gush-a-gush-a-gush-gush-gush-gush-splurt,
(reaching action)

We pump it out and barrel it,
(with both hands pretend to pump)

Gush-a-gush-a-gush-gush-gush-gush-splurt,
(reaching action)

With our crude we're really a hit,
(clapping action)

Gush-a-gush-a-gush-gush-gush-gush-splurt.
(reaching action)

Costumes and Props

Students: Wear pajamas or full length nighties. Trim with garland. Put garland in hair.

Coffee Machine, LLama, Oil Rig: Obtain three large moving boxes (the size of a refrigerator). Cover all four sides with different colored mural paper. Leave three sides undecorated. Make a transparency of the patterns and enlarge them to fit on the side of each box. Paint sketches. Trim with garland.

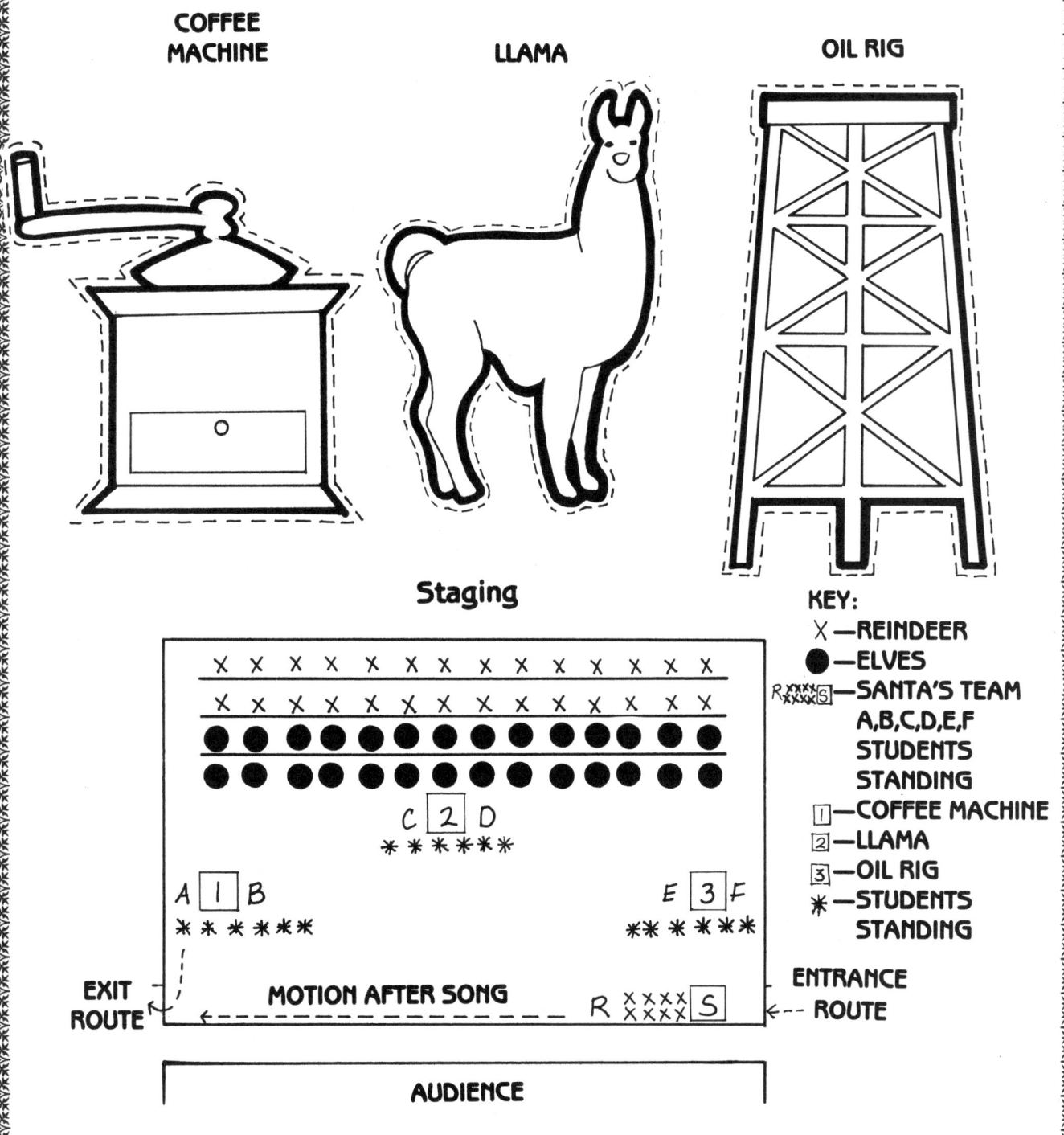

North American Professions

1. Santa reaches into his sleigh and pulls out poster #7, "Howdy, North America!" He shows the poster to the audience, pretends to get a few presents out of his sleigh and takes his place back in the sleigh.
2. Enter students and take their positions on stage.
3. Sing song twice while doing actions.
4. At the end of song, Santa is pulled to middle of stage.
5. Students stay in positions on the stage. They then sit down.

Song #9
North American Professions
(sung to the tune of "Thirty-Two Feet and Eight Little Tails")

Barbers, plumbers, nurses, painters,
Teachers, lawyers, farmers, butchers
Are just to name a few.
In North America, it's sure great to choose
What profession you would like to do.
Doctors, dentists, politicians,
Lifeguards, actors and beauticians
Are just to name a few.
In North America, it's sure great to choose
What profession you would like to do.
Off to work we go—
Barbers cutting, plumbers fixing, actors on their shows.
Athletes, artists, store clerks, bakers,
Mailmen, fishermen and dancers
Are just to name a few.
In North America, it's sure great to choose
What profession you would like to do,
'Cuz there's always one just right for you.

Actions

Barbers, plumbers, nurses, painters,
(march, swing arms in time to the music)

Teachers, lawyers, farmers, butchers
(march, swing arms)

Are just to name a few.
(both arms extended upwards in a V formation)

In North America, it's sure great to choose
(both arms extended out to audience)

What profession you would like to do.
(point to self with both thumbs)

Doctors, dentists, politicians,
(march, swing arms in time to the music)

Lifeguards, actors and beauticians
(march, swing arms)

Are just to name a few.
(both arms extended upwards in a V formation)

In North America, it's sure great to choose
(both arms extended out to audience)

What profession you would like to do.
(point to self with both thumbs)

Off to work we go—
(jog in place)

Barbers cutting, plumbers fixing, actors on their shows.
(pretend to cut, pretend to fix, pretend to act)

Athletes, artists, store clerks, bakers,
(march, swing arms in time to the music)

Mailmen, fishermen and dancers
(march, swing arms in time to the music)

Are just to name a few.
(both arms extended upwards in a V formation)

In North America, it's sure great to choose
(both arms extended forward to audience)

What profession you would like to do,
(point to self with both thumbs)

'Cuz there's always one just right for you.
(march, swing arms in time to the music)

Costumes and Props

North American Professions

Students dress up to represent all the professions mentioned in the song. Trim all outfits with garland.

Examples:

Painter: Wear paint clothes, a painter's hat, carry brush and pail of paint.

Teacher: Wear horned-rimmed glasses, carry a yardstick or a textbook.

Doctor: Wear white lab coat and stethescope.

Lifeguard: Wear a swimsuit and carry a buoy.

Plumber: Wear work clothes and carry a plunger.

Banners: Each student wears a banner across his chest with the name of his profession printed on it. Make banners out of colored mural paper and decorate.

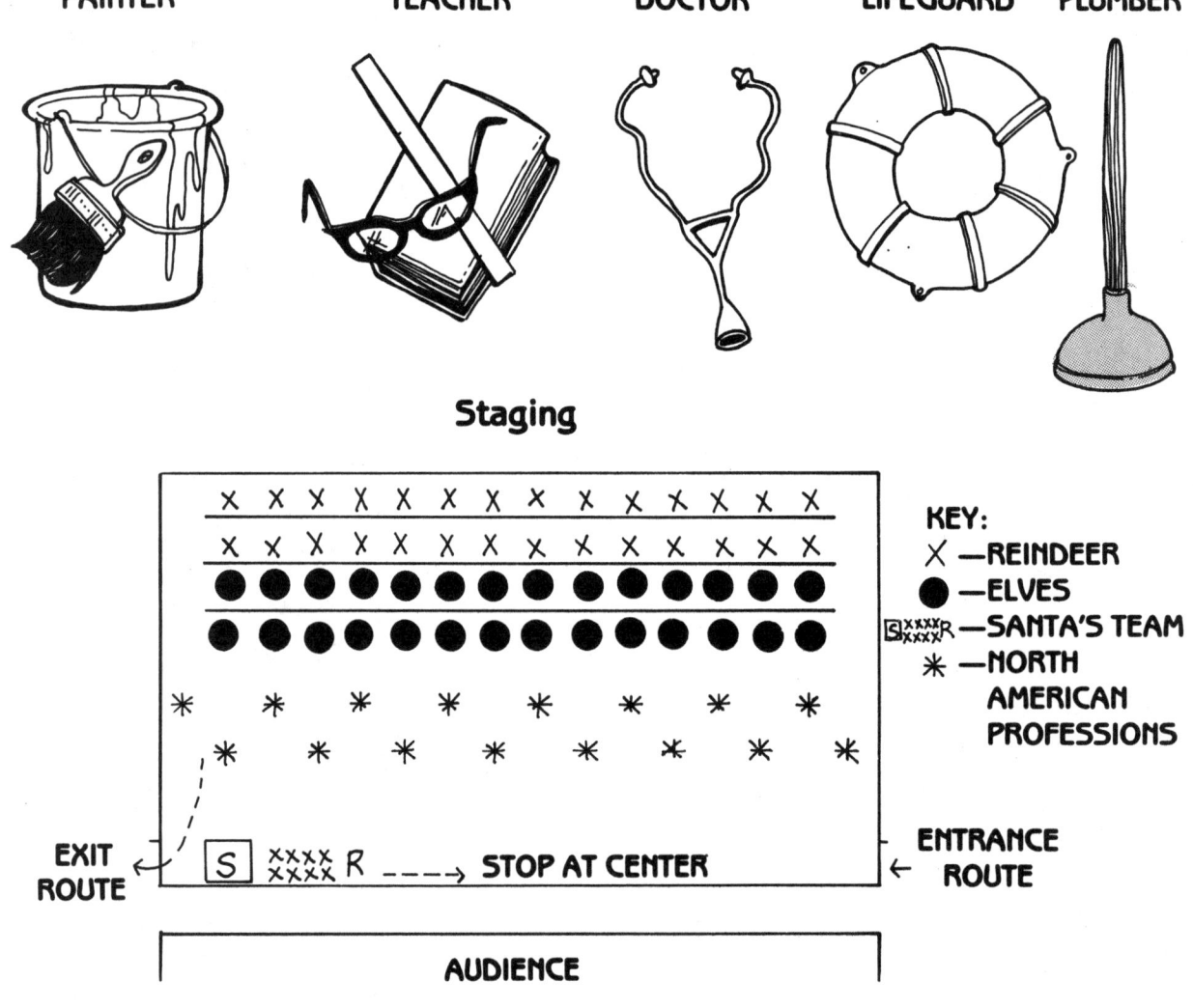

North American Cities and Finale

1. Santa remains seated in sleigh.
2. All students from entire concert come into the gym using all doors, moving quickly into position. Each carries and waves a sign with a North American city on it.
3. All students sing song through twice while moving their signs up and down in time to the music.
4. At the end of the song, Santa gets out of his sleigh and holds up poster #8, "Now it's back to the North Pole!"
5. All students sing finale verse for song #2, standing still with signs above their heads.
6. Santa waves to audience. The Reindeer and Santa leave through gym doors.
7. All students say in unison, "We Wish You a Merry International Christmas. Good Night!"

Song #10

North American Cities
(sung to the tune of "Up on the Housetop")

L.A. and Houston and Denver too,
All are cities known by you.
New York and Washington and Boston,
Naming cities in the states is fun.
U.S.A., cities galore,
U.S.A., cities galore,
Cities galore in U.S.A.,
Travel and see them and have a stay.

Vancouver, Winnipeg, Montreal,
Edmonton and that's not all,
Toronto, Regina, Ottawa,
We're naming cities in Canada.
Canada, cities galore,
Canada, cities galore,
Cities in the cold North,
Travel east and west and back and forth.

Mexico City and Mazatlán,
Are places you can get a tan.
Puerto Vallarta is lots of fun,
Mexican cities for everyone.
Mexico, cities galore,
Mexico, cities galore,
Cities galore in Mexico,
They can really keep you on the go.

Actions

For the entire song, each student will move his city sign up and down above his head in time with the beat of the music.

Staging

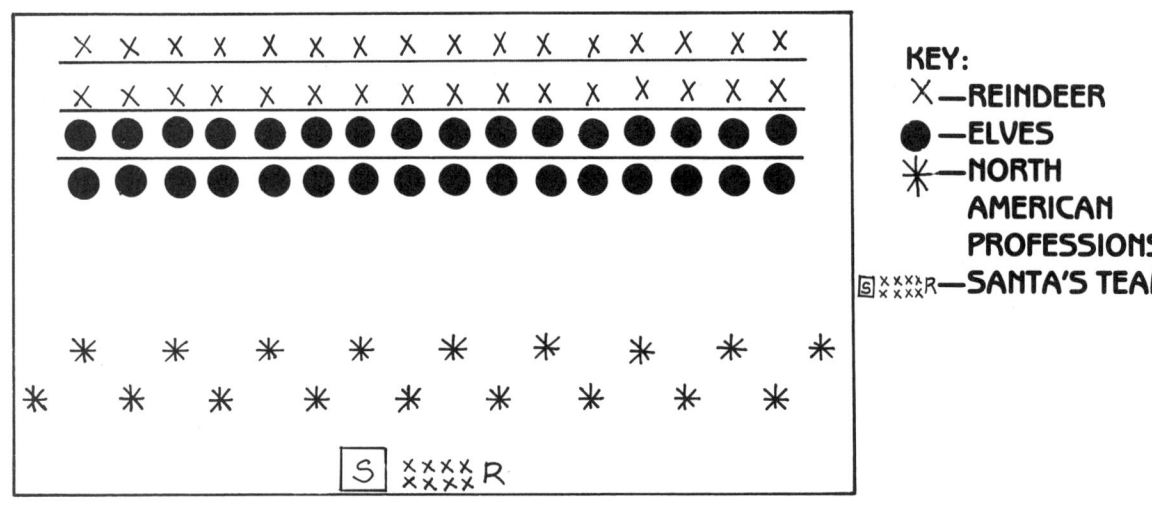

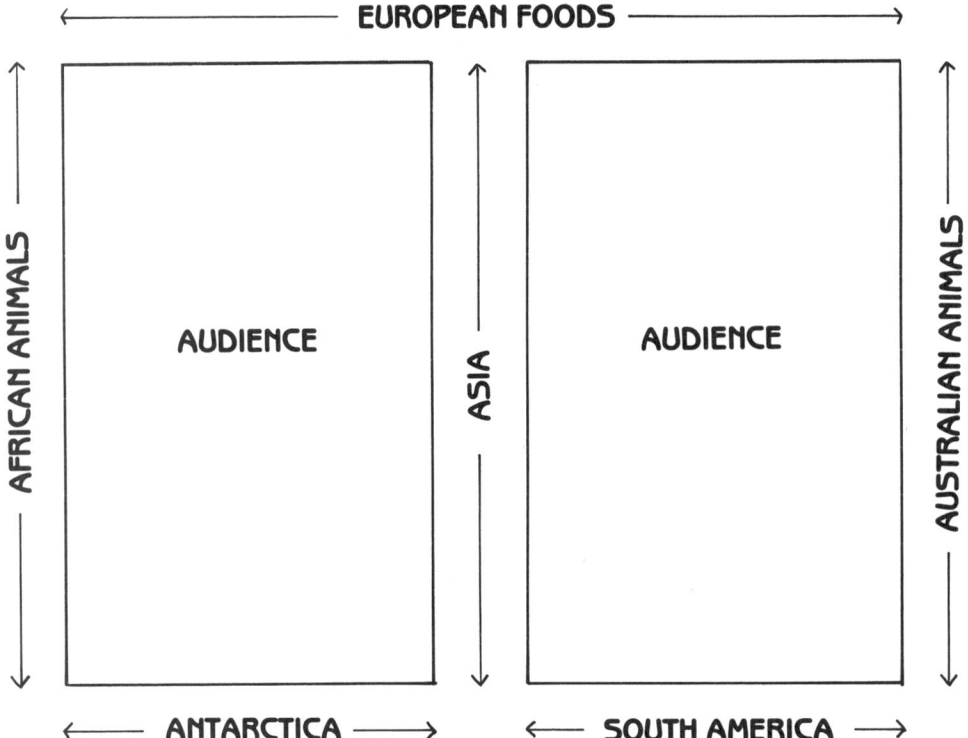

Invitations

Fill in the necessary information on ticket and duplicate one for each child to take home.

DATE OF CONCERT
TIME OF CONCERT
PLACE OF CONCERT
OPTIONAL SECTION IF HAVING REFRESHMENTS

Here's Your Ticket Around the World to Help Us Celebrate
"An International Christmas"

Your Concert Seat Is Reserved for: _____
Your Sleigh Leaves at: _____
Your Sleigh Leaves from: _____

If you have any souvenirs from countries around the world, we would appreciate your sending them to school for display purposes. They will be returned to you following our international Christmas concert.

Please bring: _____

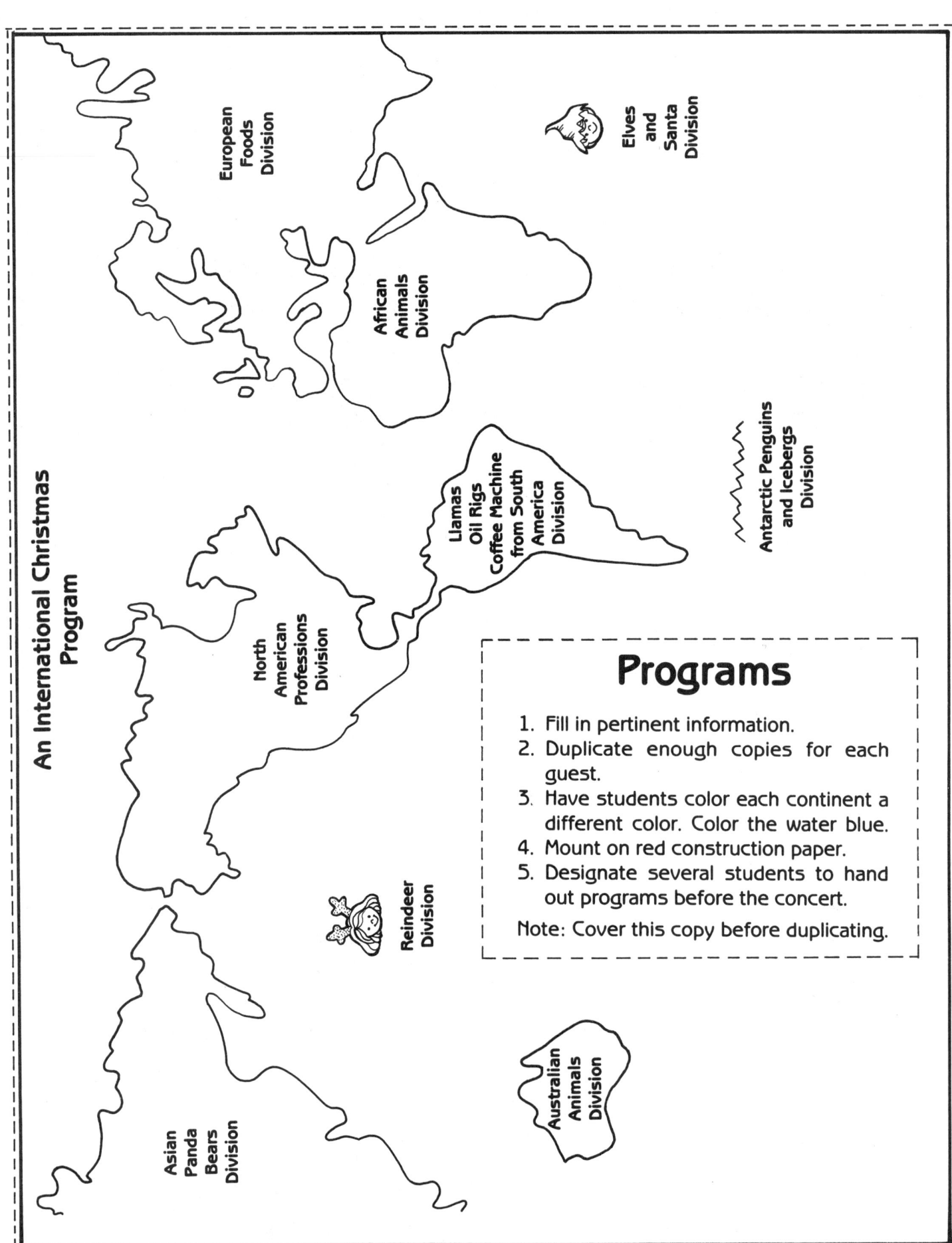

Decorations

Christmas Cards from Around the World
Obtain map outlines of different countries in the world. Trace the outlines onto an overhead projector to enlarge the outlines. Fold large pieces of colored bristol board in half and trace the outlines onto the cards. Have student locate and label major cities on the map and color. Inside, have student write an appropriate Christmas greeting. Hang on walls of gym.

Flags
Have children copy and color flags of different nations on large pieces of white drawing paper. Print the names of the countries in large letters on the backs. Hang flags from the ceiling.

Merry Christmas Signs
Make large banners with *Merry Christmas* written on them in different languages. Hang banners on the walls of the gym.

Variation: Cut out large ornament shapes and print *Merry Christmas* on them in different languages.

Display
Ask parents (via the invitation) to send in different items they have collected from different parts of the world. Display them in a central part of the school.

Refreshments

To be done by individual classes back in classroom following concert, if desired.

Each parent is asked to bring (via the invitation) one food item for the luncheon after the concert. Prepare a list of foods appropriate for the luncheon. Discuss the menu with the class and have them discuss it with their parents. Have each parent sign up to bring one item. Include paper plates, cutlery, napkins and salt and pepper on list.

Suggested Food Items

lasagna
pizza
burritos
chow mein
sweet and sour chicken wings
Greek salad
fried rice
mild curry
smoked salmon
fruit shish kebab
schnitzel
quiche
paella
sauerkraut
custard with fruit topping
Bavarian creams

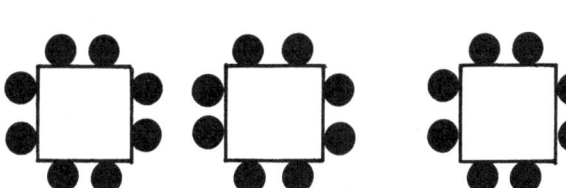

Place Mats
Have students design and color place mats for tables. Designs could include maps, landscapes or national costumes.

Aprons
Cut out apron shape and staple crepe paper strips to the waist. Have servers decorate with names of cities, maps or national costumes.

Music
Have students bring in albums containing music from different parts of the world.

Room Setup
In the center of the room set up two or three long tables to put the food on. Make a tablecloth for these tables with colored mural paper. Arrange other tables around the center tables. Place enough chairs around tables for each guest. Put place mats on table. Each table should be equipped with cutlery, glasses for children, cups and saucers for adults, napkins and salt and pepper.

Serving
Assign a group of students to serve tea, coffee and punch to each table.